THE WOLF OF WALLAN

AN EVIL MONSTER WHO PREYED ON INNOCENT CHILDREN

SUSAN BAIRD

Paperback: 978-1-967820-36-8
Hardcover: 978-1-967820-74-0
eBook: 978-1-967820-37-5
Library of Congress Control Number: 2025909029

This is a work of nonfiction.

Ordering Information:

Prime Seven Media
518 Landmann St.
Tomah City, WI 54660

Printed in the United States of America

TABLE OF CONTENTS

CHAPTER ONE
THE BEGINNING OF SILENCE

Wallan was just a small country town, the kind of place where everyone thought they knew everyone. On the outside, it looked quiet and safe. But for me, it was where my childhood ended before it had even begun.

I was five when it started. Too young to understand, too young to have words for what was happening. He was a man my parents trusted, someone who came into our home like family. To me, he was "Uncle." To them, he was a friend. To me, he became the shadow that stole my voice.

The first time, I didn't even know what it meant. I only knew that something felt wrong, something I couldn't tell my mum or dad. He told me not to speak, and I believed him. In a small town like Wallan, silence was easy. People didn't ask questions. And children weren't meant to have secrets this heavy.

The days carried on as if nothing had happened. I still went to school, still played outside, still smiled when people looked my way. But inside, I was already learning how to disappear.

I wore my silence like armour. No one could see the shame I carried. No one knew the truth I had already buried deep inside.

That was the beginning of the silence—the silence that would follow me through childhood, through school, into adulthood. A silence that would take decades to break

When I was a child; our family lived on a farm in country Victoria. I had three older brothers than me; I was the youngest and the only girl at this stage. My dad migrated from Holland to Australia where he met my mother; they began a relationship, moved in together, and had children, but never married.

Dad was always up early, milking cows and doing all the maintenance work around the farm. He was a hardworking man. At times, Mum helped Dad milk the cows; she also had a job in a café in Kalkallo, Victoria. I loved the country life and the freedom of living on the farm and having so much land to play on. I remember a time on the farm when Dad was driving the Ute to collect hay bales from the shed to feed the cows, and we were all on the back. Dad was backing back toward the hay shed, and one of my brothers saw a mouse and jumped off to catch it. Dad did not realize it and nearly squashed him. We were all yelling and screaming for Dad to stop, and he stopped just in time, it was very scary. Dad was getting sick of working on the farm; he wanted to move on, get another job, and buy their own home. They moved into a small rental room before Dad got offered to buy a house in Wallan for a good price. They were excited, and Dad jumped at the chance of owning his own home. This home had a lot of work to do, as Dad wanted to build bedrooms for us kids. The house was built on a half-acre in a very small railway town; there were only around twelve houses on the street, a general store, a pub, and a railway station. There were some people who worked on the railways living in subsidized railway housing. The general store was next to the pub; it was a small house with the shop at the front and the living quarters at the back. This town was a tight-knit community, and everyone knew each other's business. The main thing for some women was to wait until the general store opened in the morning. Rush in to get some of their daily shopping and get all the gossip about what was happening at the weekend who had too much to drink and got kicked out of the pub? Who fought in the town? And so on. This was very clear early that if you got into trouble, your parents would know before you got home. I was five when we moved into this town, and I was excited to meet friends and to start my new school. Mum said I was going to go to Wallan Primary School and that it was very small. The first day was fun; we had a nice teacher. We sat down and drank our bottles of milk that were delivered in grey milk crates. Everyone must have one. I sometimes took a different flavor of quick powder to mix in my milk to make it taste better. I would share it with my friends. As much as I enjoyed my school times, I was excited when it was time to go home. I had not had much time to discover the town that I was living in, so when I got home, it was time to start exploring. I changed out of my school uniform and went off to discover what I could get up to. I found a creek at the end of our street that had tadpoles and all sorts of bugs. At this time of the year, the grass was so green, the trees were blooming, and I very much loved it when it rained. I loved the smell of the rain when it fell on the gardens and watered the plants. I also loved the storms when the weather was fierce, as if it was telling you, it was not in a good mood. I told Mum that I wanted a bug catcher for Christmas so that I could catch tadpoles and butterflies when I was near the creek. I think my mum just wanted me to be a girly girl, but I had three older brothers all I wanted to be like them. Jeans and T-shirts made better sense to me living in the bush. We lived at the end of a narrow road, but it was not dirty; it had been tarred. Our house was like an old cottage home. The driveway was gravel, and the house looked like it was made of painted timber. Mum and Dad met a family across the road, and they seemed lovely. She was a stay-at-home mum, and her husband worked for Telecom. They had three boys of their own. Mum said that I had to call them Uncle and Auntie, so that is what they became in our lives. My dad became very friendly with Uncle and Auntie. They would talk for hours about the town, its jobs, and their future goals. Uncle was a smart man; he was the boss of one of the departments for Telecom. He always dressed well with smart dress pants, collared shirts, polished black shoes, and a big, thick black belt to hold his pants up around his belly. His hair was wavy and a little grey. He would style it with Brylcreem so it would not move. Everyone in the town warmed to his personality; he was a pillar of society and held a lot of power. Auntie was your typical stay-at-home mum. She was beautiful, kind, and compassionate; she loved her husband dearly. When my mum and I went to visit the family, I just remember thinking I wished my mum did not work and was home all the time like Auntie. They lived in a big house, and Auntie loved to bake. She always had homemade biscuits and cupcakes that had just come out of the oven. I looked forward to eating them; they were so yummy. As I got older, I started spending a lot of time at their house. Uncle and Auntie made me feel so special; they always had lollies and homemade cakes, and their house was full of love and laughter. If Mum was not home when I got home, I would rush over to Auntie's. I could smell her cooking as I got closer to her house. When we ate at Auntie's, she would decorate her table before we sat down. She had an old laminated, brown round table like a fifty-cent piece. She would decorate it with a white lace tablecloth, put her China dinnerware on the table, make everything look nice, then call for

Uncle to come inside. Auntie wore shirts and tops with a short apron tucked around her waist with beige stockings. She was much shorter than Uncle, and they looked funny together. Auntie had a combustion stove; I loved the smell of the wood burning in a country house, especially when it was raining outside. In their kitchen, they had big, long square windows over the sink, and you could see our house from there. With my mum and dad working a lot, this place was my second home, a place where I began to feel safe. Uncle had a love for horses. He had one horse when I was growing up and lots of land and a stable outback. At times, I got to pat the horse, feed him, and learn how to care for them in general. I loved the times spent with Uncle and Auntie at their house. I remember one time with Auntie, she asked if she could brush my hair and plait it, as I never really let Mum do it because it hurt so much. She seemed to love it as she never had a girl, so I persisted with it just to make her happy. As their relationship grew with my parents, they had full trust in their new family friends, and I was free to go there whenever I wanted or when Mum and Dad were not home. Time passed. We were getting older; my brothers were friends with their boys, and everything seemed to be going well in this new town we called Wallan.

CHAPTER TWO
UNCLES HOUSE

The Secrets I Carried

Growing up in Wallan, everything looked ordinary from the outside. Kids rode their bikes down country roads, families gathered at the football oval on weekends, and neighbors waved at each other in the street. It was the kind of town where nothing bad was supposed to happen.

But I carried a secret no one could see. Behind my smile, behind the chatter of a little girl who seemed fine, I was living with a shadow. He had made sure of it.

I learned quickly how to split myself in two. On the outside, I was bubbly and full of life. On the inside, I was terrified. Every time I saw him, I felt the weight of what he had already taken and the fear of what he might take again.

I wanted to tell someone. I wanted to run to my mum, to cry in her arms, to ask her to make it stop. But the words wouldn't come. He had told me not to speak. And even if I had tried, I didn't know how to explain something I barely understood myself.

So I stayed quiet. I became good at pretending. At school, I laughed with my friends and handed in my homework. At home, I played the part of a normal child. But inside, the silence grew heavier.

The worst part was not just what he did, but how he made me feel about myself. Dirty. Unworthy. Afraid. As if I was the one who had done something wrong. As if I was the one who should be ashamed.

That's the thing about secrets like mine—they don't just stay hidden. They seep into every corner of who you are. They shape how you see yourself, how you trust others, how you live.

And for me, that silence became a second skin

Uncle and Auntie's house became my second home while I was growing up. I love Auntie's homemade cooking. I could smell it as I was walking across the road from my house. I loved hearing people laughing, talking, and having fun together. I was craving so much attention, and Uncle was becoming a father figure; he gave me all the attention that I was not getting from my own father. Even when my dad was home, he had his own hobbies and liked to spend time working in his shed. I trusted Uncle, and I knew that Mum and Dad thought he was a good man, but underneath the surface lay the Wolf of Wallan, an evil monster that preyed on young girls for his own sexual pleasures. My first memory of this person who was meant to care for me and protect me was in their own home across the road from my Mum and Dad's house. I was excited one morning to go over the road to visit Uncle. My mum dressed me in a green dress. I wore long white socks with lovely white buckle shoes, and my hair was long and curly. I was five years old. I started walking toward Uncle's house; it was a cold day. I thought Auntie would have the stove going and their house would be nice and warm. And if I were lucky, she might have been baking that day. I went to the door, and Uncle answered.

"Come inside, love, and sit in the lounge," he said. "It's nice and warm in there."

"Where is Auntie?" I asked.

"She has gone out; she'll be back soon."

"It is just us until later," Uncle said.

"Okay, Uncle. I will sit and watch some TV."

"You are such a pretty little girl; why don't you come sit on my lap?" He spoke.

I went over, and he said, "Why don't you lie down on the couch and have a little rest. It is warm and cozy in here." I lay on the couch on my belly; that is how I used to get to sleep. As I was lying there, Uncle came over and sat beside the couch. He started putting his hands under my dress. He said that I was his special girl and such a pretty little thing and then started to put his fingers inside my vagina. He was rubbing them all around; that is how I explained it as a little girl. His big hands were rubbing up and down on my nipples. I was only five; I did not even have breasts. Uncle told me to lie on my side and place my bum a little bit in the air so he could see my vagina when he was rubbing it. After a while, I said to Uncle that I felt all warm and fuzzy and that it was kind of a funny feeling. He said to me that it was okay if I liked it, and this could be our little secret – a secret between only him and me, to never tell anyone, especially my mum and dad. When he finished his time with me on the couch, he went and washed his hands, came back, and sat down as if nothing had happened. I was so confused; I had not even learned about my body or had talks about sex and realized later that I had my first orgasm at the hands of Uncle. Uncle would continue this in my childhood many times as I started to grow and develop. He thought that his secret was safe, so he started to progress more with the abuse. He would tell Auntie that we were going for a drive and that he had to see one of their friends to help them out. At times, we would see people that Uncle knew, but most of the time, it was just the two of us. Uncle's car was a blue wagon, and in the front, the seat was a bench seat, so Uncle would tell me to sit up close to him. I would snuggle into his arms while he was driving. One time, Uncle and I went for a drive up to Pretty Sally Hill. There was a petrol station on the right-hand side at the top of the hill. Uncle asked me if I wanted some lollies and a milkshake. They were my favorite things to have when I was little. I said, "Yes, please."

When we sat back in the car, Uncle said, "I will take you to see all the pretty lights that overlook Hidden Valley; you can sit and eat your lollies and finish your milkshake before I take you home."

"Okay," I said, "that's nice."

We got back into his car, and he drove to a parking bay just across the road from the service station. The lights at night were so pretty. We were parked at the top of the parking bay, and it was very dark. No one was in sight. When I finished my drink and lollies, Uncle started to rub his hands inside my vagina again and slide them across my nipples.

"It's okay, love," he said. "I know it feels nice; no one will know it is our secret. You are such a beautiful little girl."

He would push my head between his legs, and my face would be lying on his penis. Uncle says that these are his secret games because I am so special, and he only shares them with me. We got home that night to Auntie's around nine o'clock. It was a cold night and dark, but Uncle just watched me run across the road to Mum and Dad', we had a long gravel drive and there were no lights, so I could not see in the dark. I felt a little scared.

I went inside. My mum was up waiting for me to get home. She asked me if I had a good time. I was not sure what to say as this was a big secret and Uncle told me not to tell. I said I was tired, said goodnight, and went to bed. Mum was always doing stuff at night for us kids—hanging washing on the line late at night, cleaning, and getting things ready for us for school. The days that I did not go over to Uncle's and Auntie's place and was not at school, I played with one of my friends. She went to the same primary school I went to in Wallan. She also lived on the same street as me. She had told me that she was adopted and was not very happy at home. We started to go over to Uncle's place, and, at times, fought for Uncle's attention. I had no idea at the time that this little girl was carrying the same secret as me. Uncle was molesting her, too. We never spoke about any of this to each other. Uncle worked for Telecom, and across the road from him was an old Telecom exchange that was not being used anymore. As he was a supervisor, he held all the keys for this building. This exchange was on the other side of the street, just up from his house. This was the perfect place for Uncle to take us. The building had a high barbed wire fence around it. The gate where Uncle used the keys to get in had a big padlock with lots of circular chains.

My mum sometimes stayed with her family in Geelong for a few days, and I would be home with Dad. When I went over to Uncle's while Mum was away, he said I could speak to my mum for free and would take me across the street to the exchange, and he would wait with me. Uncle and I walked across to the compound. He had a chain full of keys unlocking the padlocks to get into the building, then more keys to get into his office. The compound was a weatherboard building. When you walked in, there was an office that had dark, horrible carpet that smelled like mold. There was an old switchboard like you see in the movies with cables hanging out everywhere. Uncle asked me for Mum's phone number and phoned, then put the connection through to me so that I could talk to her. We could not use our phone at home as it did not have STD to call Mum. We talked for around half an hour, then I really had nothing more to say, so I said goodbye, and Uncle hung up for me. I thought that we were going to go home. Uncle asked me to sit on one of the old office chairs, so I sat for a while. I started to read the signs of his body language, the way that he would talk about me, then undo his big black belt of his pants that were just about up to his stomach, pull his pants down and ask me to rub his penis, then he said that we could play a game and if I used my tongue to lick it; this was like magic, and his penis would go hard. When I did this, Uncle would make a funny noise, and this white sticky stuff would fall on him. He said that I was so good at doing this, and I was the best out of all the girls. This time, when he was rubbing inside my vagina, I was a little sore, but I felt the tingles in my body again, and it felt warm and fuzzy. Uncle was asking me to try different things each time we were on our own. From then on, I knew when we went to the Telecom exchange, we would be playing games. The parking bay and the exchange were among many places for Uncle to abuse young girls. The next place for Uncle was in his home, where his three boys slept. This room was off their kitchen; it had a white sliding door to get into, and it was long. It had one single bed in the front room near a wall with a brown bedspread on it that covered the entire bed and draped it to the floor. At the back of the room were two single beds with the same brown bedspreads; one wasn't far from a window. Auntie was shopping with her friend Kate, and Uncle was giving me lollies and a milkshake. I was feeling a little sleepy.

Uncle told me to lie on one of the boys' beds in the back room. I must have dozed off for a little while. When I woke up, Uncle was touching me. I do not remember much this time, just woke up, and Uncle was playing with my breasts and separating my legs to look inside my vagina. Again, this was our little secret. When Auntie got home from shopping, she was happy having been out all day, and Uncle said it was time for me to go home. Because Mum and Dad worked most days, when it was a family day at my school, Uncle and Auntie would come in their place. Auntie would spend the previous day baking her homemade cupcakes and biscuits. They were my favorites. She would pack a picnic basket with white lace tablecloths and everything we wanted to eat and drink. I felt so loved and happy that I had someone at school for my family day. I loved my Auntie because she treated me like a daughter she never had, from telling me lots of stories and brushing my hair to caring for and cooking for me. I was so scared that if I told her what Uncle was doing to me that she would not believe me and kick me out of her life. That price to pay for having my Auntie in my life was too much for me to think about. Auntie was such a good cook, and she would spend hours in the kitchen. She cooked the best Sunday roast. I just adored her, as she made me feel loved. Uncle had a different way of showing me his love. Uncle's abuse went on all through my primary school years, abusing me every opportunity he got. One day, when I went to see him, he told her to visit a family member who lived within walking distance of them to have some coffee. Most times when I was at his house, he would ask her to go to the general store for something or to visit his sister, who lived just across from them. I wondered at times if Auntie ever had any suspicions, or was she curious why he wanted her out of the house when girls from the street I would visit. If Auntie was out shopping or gone for a walk with her friends,

Uncle knew that he had lots of time; at this stage, he had never have been caught. One day, when Auntie was home, Uncle said he was going to visit his dad, who lived just across from him. He knew that I enjoyed his dad's company. I called his dad Pop. Pop shared lots of stories with me. He loved company and told me all about his war days. Pop loved to collect stamps; he brought out his collection and started showing me the rare stamps that I should look for. That day, my love for stamp collecting started. Uncle would be in the kitchen with his sister, having his cup of tea and gossiping about what was happening in the town. Auntie did not really care much for Uncle's sister. She said she was nothing but a troublemaker. There were many times in their marriage when they would fight about her. Pop was getting tired, so I went into the kitchen to see Uncle. His sister wore the same sort of clothes that Auntie wore, a long skirt just past the knees and long socks that looked like brown stockings. She wore dark colored shoes that were always clean and polished. Uncle's sister also wore an apron tied tightly around her waist, and her hair was always brushed and neat. I did love fashion in the sixties. I remember being in their house, just loving the smell of the burning fire, the dirty smoke smell, and the sound of the rain on a stormy day. Uncle's sister had an old-fashioned kitchen with a combustion stove that you had to stack wood in to get it going. It was so nice and cozy and warm on a cold day. On top of the stove was a stainless-steel kettle covered in black smoke from the fire burning. Uncle said it was time to go, but that his brother had a big shed down the back of his property with lots of old cars, old Ford, and Holden cars back in the day. I had a love of cars as my dad was always working on them in my childhood, and my brothers liked old cars as well. I was excited to go with Uncle to see these special cars. We walked out the back of Pop's house, and there was a big shed with old cars in it. Uncle shut the door behind him and asked me to pick my favorite car to sit in. They were all so shiny and clean, so I picked one just because of the color that it was. Uncle came to sit in the front with me and said, "You are a pretty little girl." I felt that Uncle really did love me. Uncle told me, "Sit a little closer," and asked me to rub his penis. Hold it and rub it up and down. "You want to make Uncle happy, don't you? He said. I nodded.

Uncle started by putting his fingers in my vagina and rubbing them inside me. He did this, and, at times, rubbed my nipples. I have not developed breasts yet. He would say it was kind of magic when I rubbed. What I did not know at this age was that it was his penis. Uncle cleaned himself up, pulled his pants up, tied his big black belt around his pants, then said we needed to go home. I think we went home through the back paddock that led to his house, where there was a gate at the back to get into. Auntie seemed happy to see us. I knew that I just had to keep this secret from her. At this stage, Uncle was not threatening me, as I was doing what I was told. I was a perfect victim for Uncle, craving a father figure, just wanting to be seen and heard. Auntie and I talked for some time at their home after Pops' visit, and then it was getting dark, and it was time to run home down the street to my house.

CHAPTER THREE
UNCLES STABLE

Learning to Hide

By the time I was old enough to know something was wrong, I had already mastered the art of hiding. I hid my fear behind laughter. I hid my shame behind loud words. I hid myself so well that no one thought to ask if I was okay.

In a small town like Wallan, people noticed if you were late to school or if your grades slipped. But they didn't notice the way I froze when he walked into a room. They didn't see how I held my breath when I heard his car pull up. They didn't see the way I flinched at a touch that looked harmless to everyone else.

I learned quickly that survival meant pretending. If I laughed loud enough, no one would hear the silence inside me. If I acted tough, no one would see how fragile I felt. It worked. Teachers saw a girl who was cheeky but bright. Friends saw someone who always had a joke. No one saw the broken pieces I carried.

But the act came at a cost. Every smile was a mask that left me exhausted. Every lie I told myself—I'm fine, it's nothing, don't think about it—pushed the truth deeper down. And the deeper I buried it, the heavier it became.

The hardest part was how normal it all looked. To the outside world, he was trusted, respected, even liked. To me, he was the reason I couldn't sleep at night. But I couldn't speak. In Wallan, silence was safer.

So I kept hiding. I hid behind schoolwork, behind laughter, behind the walls I built around myself. Hiding became the only way I knew how to live.

Uncle taught me a lot about horses; he had a horse that had been in the family for a long time. Uncle said that she was very friendly and a good horse to learn to ride, so I was excited to learn to ride her.

I was older now, around twelve, and Uncle started teaching me first how to look after Missy by learning to brush her hair, mixing up her food with hay and molasses. When mixed, it smelled so bad, it was like a sticky syrup. At times, we would spend hours in the stable. I would be cleaning up Missy's poop, and Uncle would be fiddling with stuff on the bench in there. I used to brush Missy's hair on her face and whisper in her ear that Uncle was a bad man sometimes. He does bad things to me and says I cannot tell anyone. I know that Missy saw the pain and fear in my eyes. I felt like she could hear everything that I said. Auntie never came near the stable or the yard unless she yelled at him to come in for dinner, so we were always on our own. I learned to put the saddle on Missy and how to tighten it when she was not pushing her stomach out. I could put the reins on her face, but I had not ridden her yet. Uncle would saddle her up for me and sit me on her, then walk me around the paddock to get me used to riding in the saddle. We would do this several times at the weekends. I never had any riding gear of my own, as they were expensive to buy. Uncle promised me that he would buy me a helmet, and Mum and Dad bought me some riding boots. All I had left to buy were some jodhpurs. I brought some with my money from working with my mum. One day, we were in the stable, and Uncle started touching me again. I was a little older, and I started to tell him that I did not want to play his games anymore. I said that I had started to like boys, and I knew what he was doing was wrong. I should have said nothing. Uncle got angry, and I became very fearful that he was pulling my arms to sit me on the bench. I did what I was told. Uncle started inserting something in my vagina. I was too scared to look at what it was. I think it was something that he took off the bench in the stable. I was sitting on the bench, and my legs were apart. Uncle was looking down there and doing something. I had learned now that I could pretend that I was out of my body and separate my mind from my body. I never really knew what Uncle was going to do when he became angry. I do not remember a lot about that afternoon in the stable, just that things were different. Uncle was getting angry with me if I did not, please him, and I started being interested in boys. He did not like that. Uncle saddled up, Missy told me to put my foot into the stirrup and put my leg over to sit in the saddle. I did it and felt proud of myself. Uncle led Missy by the reins and walked into the paddock next to his house. I was hanging with a firm grip on the reins like Uncle taught me to when I turned my head slightly to see Uncle. He grabbed my hands and threw them up in the air with mine and the reins and said that I wasn't doing it right. Now, his fist hit my mouth, and I started to bleed. Uncle said he was so sorry. He did not mean it.

"That's okay, Uncle, I will hold it properly this time."

I started to walk with Missy, then Uncle smacked her hard on her flank. She took off like a bullet heading toward Uncle's fence. The saddle had slipped around Missy's stomach, and I went with it. I was crying on the ground and found its hard to breathe. Uncle came over to me. He could not stop laughing. The more I struggled to get onto my feet, the more Uncle laughed. I think Uncle liked being in control. I think he wanted to scare me. Every time we went back into the house, he was different toward me. I would say to myself that what Uncle was doing was all my fault. Did I do something wrong or wear something wrong? Uncle was a foster carer. He and Auntie did emergency care on some weekends. I often wanted to ask the girls if Uncle had played games with them, but I was too scared that they would say something to him, then I would get in a lot of trouble. We went for a walk one day with Uncle around his property. My little girlfriend and I were with him. I was only five and had never learned to swim. Uncle was laughing and messing around as we discovered what was on his land. We seen the dam and run over to get closer to the water. Uncle picked me up and threw me in. I could not swim; he and my friend were laughing when I was choking on the dam water. I tried to keep afloat and make my way to the edge of the dam. The dirt on the banks was soft and kept falling away when I tried to get out. I felt sick to my stomach. Uncle laughed about this for years. Even when he was interviewed on *A Current Affair* about sexually abusing us girls, he found it very funny when asked about throwing me in the dam when I was five.

From when Uncle met my parents, he was eager to help them out with anything that they needed. Dad spent a lot of time at work, so if we kids were sick and needed help, Uncle would drive us wherever we needed to go. The abuse at the hands of Uncle went on from when I was five years of age until I was between thirteen and fourteen. There was a time when I was at Uncle's house and Mum and Dad were out doing stuff, I think they went shopping in Coburg, Mum loved it there, sometimes her sister Auntie Eadie would go with them too. It is confusing what happened that day, as I remember bits and pieces of that evening. I remember having lollies and my favorite drink. Auntie was there, and then she was not. I am not sure what was happening; I just knew that I went home that night, and I was frightened as Mum and Dad were not home yet. I walked across the road to my home. Uncle was watching me until I got into the drive. We had a dog called Scooby, who was on the chain down the back of our house. Mum and Dad put him on the chain when they went out if there was no one else at home. I walked down the back to get Scooby off the chain and bring him inside with me. I had a shower and scrubbed myself clean. I felt dirty that night, as if Uncle had raped me. I stood underneath the water for what felt like hours. I placed my hands on top of my head and started to pull out my hair. I had a bit of my hair in my hands, and I wanted to cut myself. I needed to realize some of the pain that I had been feeling, but I was having trouble remembering everything that happened that night. From that night on, my life was about to change. I had a secret that would shatter people's lives in this small country town. I did not want to lose the relationship that I had with Auntie, so I kept quiet. I was in year ten at school, getting straight A's, being a good student, respectful, and well-behaved. I got honor certificates at the end of every year for three years. Then came the impact of keeping this secret; my grades started to drop, my behavior was bad, and I started to binge drink. I blamed myself for Uncle's abuse. I deserved it, I said to myself. Who would believe me when Uncle was a well-respected member of our community with a powerful job and a loving wife to support him. I dropped out of school, did not finish year ten, and everyone in the community wrote me off. I was a troubled teenager and would only end up pregnant and ruin my life. Little did anyone know that it was Uncle, my mum and dad's dear, trusted friend, who had been abusing me for years, and I could not take it anymore. I had no idea how many girls were abused by Uncle, and I had no idea at this time that my sister was being abused by Uncle, as well as one of my school friends.

CHAPTER FOUR
CRACKS IN THE CHILDHOOD I NEVER HAD

From the outside, I still looked like any other kid in Wallan. I went to school, rode my bike, hung out with friends. But inside, the cracks were already showing.

I was restless in class, drifting in and out of lessons. Teachers saw a girl who was cheeky, distracted, sometimes difficult. They never saw the nights I lay awake, staring at the ceiling, praying he wouldn't come near me again. They never saw how heavy it felt to carry a secret bigger than me.

I laughed louder than I needed to. I swore more than the other kids. I played the part of the troublemaker because it was easier than being seen as weak. What no one realised was that it was all survival.

Home wasn't safer. The tension in the house mixed with the silence I carried. I loved my family, but I couldn't tell them the truth. Every time I wanted to speak, his voice stopped me. Don't tell. No one will believe you. This is our secret. And I stayed quiet, believing him.

The cracks widened as I grew. I began to feel older than my years, carrying a weight no child should ever carry. I didn't know how to be carefree anymore. I didn't know how to just be a kid.

Looking back now, I see it clearly: my childhood was never really mine. It had been stolen, piece by piece, by a man who smiled to the world while destroying me in silence.

The cracks in me were already deep. And no one saw them.

When I dropped out of school, I was fifteen and had already experienced more than anyone should have at that age. I had no self-worth, and I wanted to hide my body by covering up everything. Never would I wear bathers or show my body. I hated my skin with passion; it was terrible. The town had branded me a slut, sleeping around with people, and a waste of a life. I thought to myself, the only one who was sleeping with me and taught me how to have sex was my dad's friend. I tried to numb my trauma with alcohol. When I tried to have sex when I met a boy I liked, I was frigid. My muscles would freeze, I felt horrible. So then, in such a small town, the word was that I was frigid, and then who was the person who could sleep with me. Uncle took away how special sex was meant to be for me; he took away the belief in myself that I was worthy of someone special. I had learned not to love myself, so who else was going to want me? I was damaged goods, I thought to myself. I was uncomfortable around crowds, especially men. I thought that sex was the only thing that they wanted, not a courtship and getting to know each other first. Uncle robbed and stole my childhood from me, and my ability to have a relationship, as I felt I was not worthy of a space in this world. I left home at fifteen and moved into a caravan park with a friend. I was not old enough to get the dole as I still should have been at school. My friend was getting benefits and was paying for the rent in the caravan park. When I left home, I was feeling very broken and had learned not to feel any emotion. I hated it when people hugged me. It was so uncomfortable for me. I did not want to feel anything in my life; this was my protection. If I could say how I felt when I left school and left home, and Uncle was not touching me anymore, I would say I lost who Susan was. Who was I? To me, my skin was dirty, and my body was disgusting. I let my family down. I would never be worthy of love. Drinking became my escape. I wanted people to like me, but I didn't like myself. I would go out, pretend that I was happy, get drunk, and be the life of the party and give everyone something to talk about. I just wanted attention, someone who saw something in me. I never showed my true self. I just liked it when everyone thought I was funny and the life of the party. I was trying to survive when I left Wallan. I learned to survive by not trusting anyone. I had been taught by Uncle that sex did not have a meaning. It was just something that you did to please men. I had such a distorted outlook on life. At times, when my pain was intense, and I wanted to feel something in my body that reminded me that I was still alive, I boiled the kettle and poured it over my wrists until I felt something. If I cut myself, to me, it was a scar that was left on my body as an escape. I would pretend that everything Uncle did to me, I was releasing it from my skin. This did help me short-term. The more I practiced being happy around people, the easier it became to lie and keep my secret hidden. I tried to have sex with a boy and thought that if I drank a lot of beer, my muscles would relax and maybe I would enjoy it. I got drunk that night, and I really liked the person I had met. He was so gentle and sweet and did not live far away from me. I tried, but I thought to myself, this moment should have meant something to me; it should have been special. My body was stiff. I was frigid, and my mind went straight back to Uncle. How I felt when he forced me to do things, how confusing it was. Was I ever going to let my body relax enough to explore sex? I wanted my day in court to face Uncle to let him know that he didn't break me, and that I was still standing. This time, he is no longer in control of anything or anyone. Finally, this man was being made accountable for his crimes. He could not talk his way out of this one.

The investigation took four years to finally charge Uncle with many counts of child sexual abuse. There were six of us ready to testify to finally have a voice. I flew from Perth to Victoria to make a statement at the Wallan police station. My sister made hers in Geelong, Victoria, and the other girls made theirs where they were living at the time. One of the girls had corroborated my statement of Uncle throwing me in the dam on his property. He watched me choking on the dam water and trying to get to the banks of the dam to save myself. I knew that he was close to being charged, but I was not sure how that was going to happen. I was still living in Perth, Western Australia, but I was in contact with someone who knew when the police were going to his house. Auntie was in a home with dementia in Shepperton. Uncle was living on his own, and the officer in charge of the investigation was from the Seymore police station. She had also taken my statement. I knew when they went to his house, he would put on his bullshit charming face and say it was all a misunderstanding. Not this time, mate, you are stuffed: they have so much shit on you know you will spend your last days in prison. How I wished I could have been there to see the look on his face with plainclothes detectives in his house. My friend was watching from across the street. Uncle must not have answered the door, so they proceeded to go around the back of his property and, bingo, there he was, standing like a pillar of society, asking what he could do for them. Come down to the station and talk about these charges against you; I am sure he thought he would be able to sort this out and be home within the hour. He was charged with historic child sexual abuse by six girls in this country town and was waiting for his first court hearing. His first hearing was in the Magistrate's court in Shepperton, Victoria. There was no need for us to attend. I wanted to, and so did my sister and some other girls, to see his face and how serious this was for him now. We booked a room in a hotel in Shepperton, and the next day, we showed up at the court hearing. We just had to wait for his turn. My mum, sister, and my friend from school, also another victim of Uncle's, were there.

It was Uncle's turn to go in. I was standing near the door to the courtroom as he walked toward me. For the first time in my life, I looked at him, and there was nothing inside of me, no fear, and no warm blood running through my body. He just looked like a dirty old man who was trying to portray himself as old and sick, too old to spend the rest of his life in jail. His hair was grey now. He held his head to the side as he did when I was a young girl. I stared at him, looked him straight in his eyes, and wondered how he was feeling now no longer had any control over the outcome of the charges against him. The police officer from Seymour came shortly after we arrived. She saw us and said that we did not need to come. I would not have missed this day for the world. When the judge asked him if he was guilty or not guilty. GUILTY, your honor. We clapped and cheered. I could not hold back the tears, but it was not over yet. They set another court hearing in a few months. I felt like we had a victory for this moment, anyway. He walked out of the courtroom past us and never turned his head our way once. My mum, sister, and I then went out for some lunch to process what had just happened before returning home to Wallan. I wanted people to know about Uncle and sent our story through to A Current Affair in Victoria. They aired it on the sixth of August 2014, calling the episode THE WOLF OF WALLAN the interviewer being Martin King. We girls were nervous, so we all stuck together and supported each other, telling each other that this was our chance to have a voice. We found strength in each other; we had been keeping the same secret for decades. The show had taped the episode with us girls and their TV crew. Then the next step for them was to interview Uncle in the small country town were I lived. There were times when he would go to Wallan to do his shopping, but if he was out, he would leave his roller door up. When the TV crew got there, his roller door was up, so they rang me, and I said he would not be far away, so just wait somewhere until you see his blue wagon car drive in the driveway. They drove up the end of his street, not too far away but far enough for him not to see. Uncle pulled into his driveway and was about to get his shopping out of his car. Out came the camera crew and with microphones everywhere. Uncle did not know what was happening, and the cameras were rolling. Martin confronted Uncle by saying how he had ruined our lives. He carried his posture the same way when he was cornered and had to bullshit to get away with things. His head tilted to the side, his hand on his chin like he was confused about something. Martin asked him about throwing me in the dam when I was five years old. Uncle's response was, we have laughed about that for years. I was not laughing; I had been taking Valium on and off for years. Once they got Uncle's story, the show was aired, and most people in the town saw it. Some people were haters of us girls and said some nasty things online, and others were proud of our strength and courage to finally bring this man to justice. Either way, there were mixed emotions, although Uncle had already pleaded guilty in a court of law to several child sexual abuse acts. I decided not to read any more negative responses that were responding to the show. After the show was aired, Uncle proceeded to live his life as normal; he carried on in his normal life, doing shopping in Wallan for his groceries. He was shunned by the locals and told he was nothing but a pedophile, and they moved their children away from him. From then on, Uncle had his followers and people who did not really care or want to be involved in something like this. My own father was one of these people. He was one of Uncle's dear friends until the very end. When the police were collecting statements from us girls and anyone who was mentioned in the statements, Dad and Mum were asked to make a statement and saw Uncle's charges. The police went to see my dad in the house that I grew up in. He was with his new family now: his wife and two young boys. The police officer walked in with another officer and proceeded to talk to Dad and show him exactly what Uncle had been doing to us since we were five years old. My dad got angry and told them that he wanted nothing to do with it. It was too messy, and why didn't we speak up years ago when this was happening? They were speechless as to how a father could react to his children being sexually abused. Did he go over to Uncle's like any other father and rip his head off? No, he continued to have a relationship with him up until the day he died. In fact, he spoke to Uncle on the Sunday before his sentencing. He had a coffee with my dad, and Uncle said this is the last time that you will be seeing me. My dad asked why that was, and Uncle looked a little confused. Uncle answered that they had too much shit on him, meaning he was going to jail for his sins, and he knew it. In the next few days, I got a phone call from the police at Seymour police station saying that Uncle was dead; they had found him on his property in Wallan. I could not believe this. The gutless coward got a life sentence, and he knew that he would not survive in prison, being in his late eighties. I felt a lot of emotions. I had planned everything that I was going to say to him when he was in prison. I had written an impact statement that I wanted to read in court. I wanted closure for myself. He stole my childhood and died, so he did not have to spend one day in jail. To me, Uncle, you will always be rotten to the core, always the evil monster of Wallan.

CHAPTER FIVE

Before the Courtroom

In the weeks leading up to the court case, I felt like I was carrying a boulder inside my chest. Every day, I told myself I could do it—that I could stand there and speak the truth. And every night, doubt whispered back: What if they don't believe you? What if your words aren't enough?

I had kept his secret for so long. Breaking it open felt terrifying. For years, silence had been my safety, my shield. Speaking was stepping into danger all over again. The courthouse itself was cold and unfamiliar. People moved through it as if it were just another day at work. For me, it was the day my whole life would be laid bare. I wasn't just bringing a statement; I was bringing my childhood, my fear, my shame—all the parts I had locked away.

I remember sitting outside the courtroom, my hands trembling, my mouth dry. Faces blurred around me. The only thing I could hear was my own heart, pounding like a drum. Every step that had led me there—every night awake in silence, every time I had swallowed the truth—came rushing back.

I knew I had a choice: stay silent, or finally speak. And I also knew silence had cost me too much already.

When they called my name, I stood. My knees shook, but I walked forward anyway. I didn't feel strong, but I was. Because strength isn't the absence of fear—it's moving through it.

I was about to read words that would break open the life I had hidden. I was about to face him with the truth he had stolen from me.

And in that moment, I promised myself: I will not be silent anymore.

The second court date was at the county court in Shepperton, Victoria. This was the one where all of us girls could sit in a room and use the TV to read our impact statement. We were talking about who was going to go first, as this was upsetting for all of us. I had been taking Valium to cope, so it was decided that I would go first. Uncle's lawyer and our officers were in a meeting with Uncle. This seemed to go on for a long time. We were told that this would take a few hours to get some lunch. They would ring when it was time to go back to the court. We all went for lunch together, supporting and caring for each other. I had a few stiff drinks and was ready to confront Uncle but not have to be in the same room. The judge was going to hear all of us without having to see Uncle. We got the call to go back to the courtroom. Julie, the police officer who took my statement, came to speak to us. Uncle had decided to take a plea bargain with the lesser charges of sexual abuse being dropped. So, we all went home and waited for him to be sentenced. I had been working on my impact statement and what I wanted to read out to Uncle, hoping that from that day, he would go to jail. I never knew what Uncle's plea was for my case. I was one of four girls who had pressed charges against Uncle.

Uncle had been abusing me for over ten years of my life, and this is what he pleaded guilty to. In relation to Susan Baird, the accused entered please guilty of the following: Gross indecency x2, touching of breasts and vagina when watching TV in the living room. Indecent acts x2 charges 2 occasions where the accused inserted an unknown object into the victim's vagina. I act indecently by inserting fingers into her vagina at Telcom. The 2 occasions where an unknown object was inserted will be included in the one charge on the indictment, given their similarity to the indictment will contain 4 charges relating to Baird, through the summary will allege details of 5 charges he pleaded to. Further, the opening will include other occasions where the accused rubbed the complainant's vagina as uncharged acts. These Admissions were on the 31st of July 2014 at 12:32 p.m. I was judged all my life for dropping out of school, binge drinking, and being the talk of this small town. Never was I a bad person. I was just learning to survive, and as I grew older, I found different ways to survive. Uncle, you did this to me and many other little girls in this small town. You were an evil monster who did a lot more than you were charged with. I wanted to read you a statement on how you impacted my life; you stole my childhood. I finally wanted to stand in the courtroom and look you in the eyes without fear in mine. Your life was in the hands of the court system; you were the one vulnerable this time, old, sick, and now having to pay for your crimes.

Uncle, you have a pool of young children for your own sexual pleasure without any remorse or guilt. You portrayed yourself in this town as a respectful, kind, and caring man. A man who would do anything for anyone, especially my parents, when you had their trust. I was putty in your hands, and you did some cruel things that you did not get charged for. I endured physical, mental, and sexual abuse at your hands that will haunt me forever, but I am still standing. Uncle, you did not break me. Seeing a pathetic old man walking into a courtroom brought a smile to my face. People who you thought were on your side were in the courtroom to see justice being served.

CHAPTER SIX
(MY SISTER TRACEY'S CHAPTER)

I felt like an only child growing up. My brothers and sisters were a lot older than me. They were in their teens, while I was only five. They were off playing together. I was playing with my toys. I can only remember a few happy memories of my childhood. The rest of my memories are details of my sexual abuse. My sister and I weren't close when we were younger. We used to fight over lots of things. I wanted to watch cartoons; she wanted to watch video hits. It seemed like she was always angry at me. I thought she hated me. Little did we know that we were both dealing with the horrible secret of being sexually abused by Uncle. Always in fear that our parents and brothers would be killed or hurt if we didn't do as we were told. My best friend was Uncle's youngest son. We played with toys, cars, pretended to drive old bombs, and climbed trees. I was a bit of a tomboy, but I still played with my Barbie dolls. I loved my cats, and I had a rabbit as well. I called this man Uncle, not because he was related to me, but because he was my parents' friend. Our neighbor. In their eyes, he was a good man.

I can remember a time when I got sick with bronchial pneumonia, and he rushed me to the hospital. My mum was so grateful to him. She couldn't drive, and my father didn't think I was that sick at the time. I nearly died I think I was around five when Uncle started to touch me. My mum and I left Wallan when I was ten, so the abuse probably lasted for about five years. I can remember a lot of details about the abuse, but I have blocked out some of the more violent occasions.

I have just started counselling now, in my forties. When I went to the victim's assistance agency, they suggested it.

At first, I didn't want to go. I thought people who went to counselling were crazy. I didn't know what I was feeling myself as I had never opened myself to anyone before. How was I going to do this? I rang my sister, crying. The pressure had gotten to me. My routine was changing. I didn't like it. She said give it a go. If you don't like it, you can stop. You don't need to worry. They are there to help. She told me about some of her sessions. She made me laugh. She always makes me laugh. She always makes me feel happier.

I think when people describe me, they say I am a happy girl. Always smiling, always cheerful. I have pretended that I have been okay all this time. I wouldn't allow myself to think about anything else. I don't know why. I just did my daily routine day after day. Like a robot, doing as I was told. Being a good girl.

I lived my life, not telling many people about what happened to me. I never really had any close friends. I guess I thought that no one would care what I was feeling. What happened to me was not important. I felt unworthy of anyone's love or respect. I had no identity of my own, no personality. I would always mimic other people's personalities. I can't even cry or show any emotion because I think I don't deserve to. I can't even hug people. It is so alien to me. I drink too much, but it helps me relax, helps me show my emotions more than when I am sober. I have trouble trusting people, especially men. I get scared and anxious if I'm alone with any man I'm not familiar with. I'm scared of everything all the time. I have trouble socializing and communicating what I want to say to people. I can't stand up for myself, and I'm always trying to please everyone. I'm on guard all the time, and I never let my defenses down. I live in fear. Fear of my future, fear of my past.

I haven't lived my life like I should have. I have let so many opportunities pass me by, simply because I was scared. The only place I felt safe was in my room watching TV and movies. Escaping into the perfect stories and fairytale endings within. I would always dream about the movies I had seen, but I would put myself in the leading role and add to the story. I was always disappointed when I woke up and realized it wasn't real.

All my life, when invited to parties, I was always off talking to pets or finding a quiet spot by myself away from crowds. I had nothing worthy to say, no social skills to communicate. No one tried to talk to me. I think my face would show a frown and say *"Don't come near me.*

I didn't date until my late twenties. I had a couple of dates, but I was always thinking of a way out before they started. I just couldn't face it. I always had a sick feeling in my stomach, and it never played out like it did in the movies that I loved so much. It was safer in my room. It wasn't until my early thirties that I ran into an old work friend. We went out to catch up and ended up kissing. It was the first time I felt safe with a man. We clicked. It was the first time I hadn't felt awkward or scared of what was going to happen. It felt natural to love him. We got married and have been together for over ten years. He has helped me in so many ways. He has never rushed or forced me. He has been so gentle. He says I've been hiding under a rock for thirty years, and now I've come out. He is always making me laugh, and now I don't seem to take life too seriously anymore. We tried for children, and I did fall pregnant in my early forties but miscarried at six weeks. I had left it too late. The fear has stopped me again.

And it never dawned on me that all this was a result of being sexually abused as a child. People might say, "Why didn't you tell on him?" Well, I did, I was about six or seven and Mum was dressing me after a bath. She noticed that I was red around my vagina area and asked me what happened. I told her uncle did it. She raced me to the doctor, but there was no conclusive evidence to prove what I said was correct. A family member confronted Uncle, but he said it was all just a misunderstanding. That was that I can't remember if he touched me after that, but I do know I wasn't allowed to go over there for a while, and I missed playing with Uncle's youngest son. So, eventually, all was forgotten, and I was allowed to go over and see my best friend. I didn't go to Uncle's house to see him or the horses, or the treats. I went there to play with my best friend. When I went over there, there was always Auntie and their youngest son, my best friend. Uncle would always send them away. He would say to Auntie, "Go to the shops," and to his son, he would say in an angry voice, "Piss off". I believe they knew what was going on, but they were victims of abuse just like I was. Caught in the evil spider's web. Another time, my whole family was in Uncle's kitchen for a get-together. Mum put me in their bath so I could be ready for bed when we got home. I was playing with some toys, and Uncle came in. I froze immediately. I knew what was coming. He touched me as he pleased, and no one knew; no one came to my rescue. He had gotten away with it again.

On many occasions, he would always dress me again, afterward, all neat, and say that I was a good girl and then make me treat, like a milkshake or peel me an orange that looked like a curly worm.

There are so many other times I couldn't count them all.

I never knew I was in danger until we were alone. If I didn't do as he said, he would be violent. Once he pulled my arm hard, I was really scared of him.

My worst experience was when he talked Mum into letting him take me to the Brownies/Scouts group. He drove me there. We were alone in the car. When we got there, we did lots of fun activities during the day. The night fell, and suddenly all the women were gone. There were only men there. Everything turned dark. A sick feeling was in my stomach. I was scared and didn't feel safe anymore. Then men started molesting all the children. Boys and girls. Uncle did it to me. I can remember being near a tree outside. I blocked out the rest. I can still see all the other children, like me, powerless to stop the monsters. When I got home the next day, Mum asked how it went, and did I like it. I said I never want to go back again.

There was another time when he wanted to take me and my sister, and a group of other girls, to fly in a light plane. It sounded like such fun. I wanted to go, but I didn't want to go. He tried everything to get me to go, but I guess I knew at that time that the fun activity had a huge price at the end. My mum ended up saying that if she doesn't want to go, you can't force her. He was so angry, I just hid behind my mum's legs. God knows what my sister and the others had gone through that day. I wish that the courage that day had been there all the other times.

When it came to the police to make a statement, I felt a sense of relief. Relief that I could finally tell my story. Someone finally cared. The police were very good to me. All the bad memories had come flooding back, all at once. I cried. It was all too much. But it needed to be done. We had to finally bring him to justice.

At the court hearing, I had to come face-to-face with him. At first, I turned my back when he walked past. I just couldn't bear the thought of seeing him. By the end of the day, I had gotten my courage up. I looked him in the eye. He was old, he looked scared, and he was fragile. He was pathetic. Suddenly, I wasn't scared of him anymore. I felt empowered. I felt strong. It took all day for the attorneys to get a plea from him. I was exhausted, mentally and physically. But it was done. He had pleaded guilty. I was elated.

Then came the interview with *A Current Affair*. I was stronger. I was able to tell the world what he was, what he had done to me and many others, and how long he had gotten away with it. It was easier doing it with the other girls. We were united. We wanted justice. We wanted him to stop.

A couple of weeks later, he was dead. A heart attack, they said. Our fight for justice had ended. It wasn't the outcome I had envisioned for him. Even a week in jail would have been ideal.

But without that first plea, we would not have been able to do the interview. 5 magazines would not have been able to print its two-page story. And I wouldn't be putting my story on paper now.

So, I'm thankful for how far we have come on this journey, for justice. It has helped heal the pain and the shame I have felt all these years.

My sister and I became close after her son Martin died. She took me to the airport and gave me a hug and said, "Don't be a stranger, let's keep in contact." And we have been ringing each other ever since. We fly out to see each other when we can. She always comes to celebrate my birthday with me. One day, she said, "I'm sorry this happened to you. I'm sorry I left you."

I said, "This wasn't your fault. The only one to blame is Uncle. He did this. He is responsible."

We have slowly, over the years, been able to talk about our abuse with each other. It has been painful, but it has helped us become closer. Our bond is strong. Nothing can break it. We fight every day to be survivors, not victims.

I feel I have come a long way over the past ten years.

CHAPTER SEVEN
MY STATEMENT TO THE POLICE

Walking into the police station that day, I carried the weight of decades of silence. I wasn't just giving evidence; I was opening the locked box of my childhood. Every memory, every fear, every secret I had been forced to carry—it was all about to be spoken aloud.

I told the police how it began. How my parents trusted him. How Auntie welcomed me into their home like a daughter. How he used that trust to groom me, to single me out as his "special girl," and to convince me that what he was doing had to stay our secret.

I spoke about the car rides, the stables, the Telecom exchange, the rooms where he cornered me. I explained the confusion of a child who craved love but was handed abuse, how I felt both chosen and destroyed at the same time. I told them how I ran home some nights and scrubbed myself raw in the shower, desperate to wash him away, but never feeling clean.

As I gave my statement, the memories came in waves—the fear, the shame, the lies he told me, the silence that followed me into school, into friendships, into relationships. I told them how I carried that silence into adulthood, how it became part of me, until the day I couldn't carry it anymore.

Every word hurt. Every word opened a wound that had never healed. But I kept going, because I needed the truth on record. For so long, his voice had drowned out mine. That day, I wanted the police to hear mine clearly.

I told them he had stolen more than my body. He had stolen my childhood, my self-worth, my belief in love and safety. He had left scars that no sentence could erase. But I also told them this: he did not break me.

That statement wasn't just evidence. It was survival. It was me reclaiming the voice he had silenced.

When I finished, I felt emptied out but strangely lighter. For the first time, the truth was no longer mine alone to carry. It belonged to the world now, and to justice. That day, in that small room, I proved something to myself: my voice was finally louder than his.

CHAPTER EIGHT
AFTER THE NOISE

When the court hearings ended, when the cameras stopped rolling, and when the newspaper stories were folded away, I was left with myself. The world knew him now for what he was. The man who had been praised in our small town, respected as a friend, trusted as a neighbor—was exposed as the monster I had always known.

But once the noise faded, the silence came back. And silence has a way of feeling heavier than the shouting ever did.

I thought justice would bring closure, but closure never came. What came instead was a kind of emptiness. He was gone, but the memories weren't. The town still carried whispers, still carried judgment, still carried pieces of me I had never wanted to share.

I found myself replaying my statement, my words to the police, the look on his face when he was finally cornered. For years, I had been silenced by him. Now, I had spoken—but the question was, how do you go on after that? How do you live when the story you've carried for decades is finally out in the world?

What I learned is this: telling the truth doesn't erase the past, but it changes its weight. The secret no longer belonged to me. It belonged to the world, to justice, to history. And in that shift, I found room to breathe.

The court case wasn't the end of my story. It was the beginning of me taking my life back. Piece by piece, I started to rebuild—not as the child who had been broken, not as the teenager who had been judged, but as the woman who refused to stay silent any longer.

This was not closure. It was survival. It was the first step toward healing

After my sister shared her story, I felt relieved. We didn't really talk about each other's abuse with Uncle.

All the time that I had been married up until I knew this was going to go to court, I never shared this with my husband. I wasn't sure if I ever wanted to share this with him, but I knew that I had to before he found out from someone else.

I came home from work one evening and told my husband about Uncle and what he had done for me when I was a child. He was shocked and a little angry with me that I had kept this secret for so long and continued to allow him to have a friendship with this man. I thought, "Well, I am the shit. Now is probably a good time to share everything that happened back then." This went on for the entire evening, asking questions like I was on trial. I get it, he felt betrayed when he knew that my mum and my sister knew before him. I had told him that there were detectives coming to our house and that I just needed to be on my own for this before I flew home to Wallan to make a statement.

My husband adored Auntie; he said that she was a kind soul. Loving and caring, always willing to help anyone in need. He thought that Uncle wasn't bad either. He knew that I thought of Uncle as a father figure. Hubby and Uncle often shared beers in his home. Many times, Uncle would walk home from the pub with the locals, ask some of them back to his house, and grab Auntie out of bed with her hair to cook the boys something to eat. My eldest brother was there that night and could not believe what he was doing to Auntie. He kept on telling him to leave her alone, that we were fine and didn't want anything to eat. But he didn't listen to anyone. Auntie looked frightened and said quietly that Uncle was a pig; she often called him that.

Uncle had gone through a bad time with his drinking; he was a violent drunk, often fighting with Auntie and his children, and often in a physical punch-up. Poor Auntie, she was frightened and at times horrified as to what he was going to do next. I was over there one night when there was a scuffle. It was time for me to shut my mouth until I got to run to the door and run across the road to my home.

One night when Uncle came home from the pub with his friend, they were all very drunk. The boys were teasing him, and he said he had some underwear like a G-string. It had a trunk at the front that you tucked your penis into.

The boys went into his room where Uncle got undressed, then went into the lounge just about naked. He proceeded to stick his penis into our faces, where we were sitting on the couch in the lounge room.

He thought this was so funny, and so did the boys. Auntie was mortified. She called him a silly old fool; she was so embarrassed. I remember that night Auntie was in her dressing gown, and it was purple. My husband was laughing

and calling her the pink pimpernel.

There was a stage when Uncle seemed to be drinking a lot, but he was a violent drunk and should never have drunk at all. Even when Uncle was abusing us, if we didn't do what he wanted, we knew what was coming. Too scared of what was to come.

Many people were living in this area who had their suspicions about Uncle abusing young children, but they could never catch him in the act.

One day, they gave Uncle a good talk about what was being said around the town. They roughed him up a bit and left him on one of the old dirt roads to think about it.

It never stopped him; he continued his pattern of grooming young girls who moved into the street to abuse.

My question was, did Auntie ever know or suspect what her husband was doing?

The many times that my sister and I went over to visit, if Auntie was home or anyone else, he would ask them to go away and do something so that he could be alone doing what he wanted with us.

I went to visit Auntie in the nursing home after one of Uncle's court hearings. I was with a family member. We sat in the waiting room for her to come out to see us. It had been a long time since I had seen her, and I wasn't prepared for how Auntie looked. She was a shell of herself, and she looked so small. Inside my heart was breaking for her.

Her skin was hard; someone had brought her some moisturizing cream to rub on her arms, and this made her skin smell so nice. I got close to her ears and said, "Auntie, it's Suzie. I grew up most of my childhood with you and Uncle." She just smiled and had absolutely no idea who I was.

It really didn't matter now. I was never going to know if she ever had any suspicions about Uncle. She had dementia and had no idea who I was. I felt so sad to see someone I loved looking like she did. I had some time on my own to speak to her when the other girls were speaking to the nurses or in the restroom. I said, "Auntie, I remember all the times that you told me that Uncle was a pig. Did he do this to you? Did you find out what he was doing, and this drove you to a home?"

Her beautiful eyes just stared into mine. I loved her so much.

I then said, "Auntie, we should have hit Uncle over the head with a shovel when we had the chance and buried him in the backyard. You would have had a peaceful life then. I remember when you finally got the courage to leave him, you said I have had enough, he is a pig. I am leaving him, and you bloody did. I was so happy you moved into a place in Rosebud, Victoria. Your fear of Uncle was gone. For the first time in a long time, you look relieved.

My husband and I took a drive down to see how you were doing on your own. You said financially that you were struggling. It was tough.

I asked if Uncle had been to see her. She said that he hadn't left her alone, the constant phone calls, and the promises of him changing his life so that she would come back home.

Uncle knew how to strike when a person was vulnerable; he knew how to manipulate any situation for his own benefit. I knew that eventually she would give in to Uncle, the bastard that he was. Sure enough, when her lease was up, back she came to Uncle's home for another go at having a different life. It didn't take long before he started drinking again and being violent. I think Auntie thought that she had her chance at freedom and that she was stuck with this evil man now.

Even though I thought that Auntie was a strong lady, we all have our breaking points, and hers was dementia, a reason for Uncle to have her put in a nursing home and have the house to himself to continue his abuse.

My husband and I did get a chance to visit Auntie at their house before she went to the nursing home. Hubby had a lot of time for Auntie, just like I did. We had no idea how her memory had been so bad. Uncle said that it came in waves; she would remember at times and then have no idea. We had our daughter Melanie with us, whom Auntie had known since her birth.

My husband had sat down with Auntie and said, "Hello Auntie, it's Gary."

She said she didn't know him, but he wasn't bad looking. I was heartbroken.

"Auntie, it's me, Suzie, remember me?" I spent all my teenage years admiring the person that you were, and that is the person that I chose to remember.

After that, we really didn't see much of Auntie anymore. Only that day of Uncle's first court hearing.

MY REHAB AND COUNSELLING

I first started counselling when I was in my thirties. I thought that maybe I was ready to talk about what Uncle had done. I wasn't sure how this was going to go. I was willing to try, as Uncle was still living in my head, and I was continuing to binge drinks to cope with the demons that kept me awake at night. I first started doing this through (SARC), a sexual abuse resource center in Mandurah, Western Australia. I started my first session with a lovely lady who knew a lot about child sexual abuse. At first, I felt nervous. I was embarrassed and felt like she would look at me in a different way if I told her the truth about Uncle. It was fine; we just started talking about everything and everything around what brought me to where I was today.

In general, I said that I felt that I needed some help with understanding how I behave sometimes with other people in my world.

She said that we could work on lots of things, but at a very slow pace.

We started with one session a week, and then she went on maternity leave for a while. Then I said to myself, I had given it a go, so just go back pretending that all is good and carry on. I went on and off seeing counsellors for many years until I knew that we girls were going to court to finally have our voice. We would be seeing him in the courtroom at some stage of these hearings. I had been to my local GP for a chat about how I was feeling, and he decided to put me on valium just for a while until the trial was over. I had been on benzos in the past to help me sleep at night.

We girls stayed in Shepperton the night before the hearing. Sis and I were talking and trying to keep our minds off the trial and the fact that we would be seeing Uncle after all these years. We had each other for support, and some other family members from Uncle's family were there as well. We didn't get much sleep that night, but we were eager to get to the courtroom before Uncle got there.

All this time, I continued using benzos and alcohol, not knowing how addicted I was.

After the last hearing and finding out that Uncle had a heart attack and had passed away, I was gutted. This man was not going to spend one day of his life in jail. Uncle's family had a service for him, and he was later buried in the Wallan cemetery.

My dad and brother were buried there, too, but on the other side of Uncle.

I don't know why, but I had this pull inside me to visit Uncle's grave. I had no idea how I would feel or what my reaction would be. I just knew I was going to go there. I was still living in Western Australia, so I organized a flight home to Victoria. I said to my sister I am coming home. I am going to the cemetery to see where Uncle is buried. It had only been around six weeks since the burial, so there was just a large pile of soil placed on top with a tiny temporary tombstone that hadn't been set in yet.

My first thought was to kick the shit out of the dirt, pick up the tombstone, and throw it. But my sister was with me, and she is a lot more rational. She kept telling me that if I got caught doing anything to Uncle's grave, I would get arrested.

I had been told that by a detective involved with the case. If I got caught defacing Uncle's grave, I would be arrested. But if no one saw it would be happy days for me. I did take some toilet paper with me as there were no toilets at the cemetery, just in case I needed to go, and that is all I will say about that.

I went back home that day with my sister, then flew back home to Queensland.

I had been seeing a GP in Queensland for a while when I was living there, at first just for small issues, until I felt safe enough to talk about the court case and my childhood with Uncle. I was keen to come forward with how often I had been taking benzos and using alcohol to wash them down. No one knew how bad it was except for my sister. At Uncle's second court hearing, I had taken a few Valiums that morning to cope. And we were talking to our lawyer about who was going to speak to the judge first on the TV screen. My sister told the lawyer that I'd better go first because I had been on valium all morning. She laughed a little and told me to go first and get it out of the way. We all knew when we were going to testify.

Uncle was in meetings with his lawyer, and our lawyer was going back and forth. We were told to go and have some lunch, and they let us know when to come back.

I told my sister that I need something stronger to calm my anxiety. I couldn't stop shaking. My nervous system wasn't kind to me. Sis got me a double scotch. I said one would be fine. She laughed and said it was okay, but that was all I was having. It seemed like hours that we were waiting, then finally Uncle decided to Take a plea. What a relief not having to testify and knowing that he pleaded guilty to the worst things that he had done. Evil bastard. I wonder how he felt in a room, not being able to manipulate anyone for his own personal gain.

When I think back to when this all started with Uncle, I learned at a very young age how to survive. I learned how to separate my mind from what Uncle was doing to me. It was almost as if I could leave my body, and Uncle was just using a shell of my body for his own pleasure. I would move away from Uncle within my mind as if to me that this wasn't really happening.

For years, I have blamed the five-year-old child within me. It's almost as if she died inside to cope with Uncle's abuse. I just wanted to feel normal. My mind was wired to survive at a young age. Some of the physical abuse I remember clearly, and other times, in my mind, it is the nice things that Uncle and Auntie did that I remember. So confused as a child. I was forever on high alert with Uncle.

When I was growing up around Uncle, there were two of me. One full of bullshit, trying to make everyone believe that I was such a happy-go-lucky, bubbly person. Then the one inside of me taught me what to do to survive in my world.

Most of the time, this worked for me. I kept busy running away to avoid dealing with Uncle's shit.

There was a time when I was at Broadford High School in Victoria, where we had a swimming carnival coming up for all the houses. I think my color was a yellow t-shirt and green bottoms. I said to my mum Please don't make me go to school that day, as they were having a swimming carnival, and I did not want to go. Mum does not really understand why. The fact that after Uncle threw me in the dam, then laughed his arse off as I was struggling to save myself when I was a child, I would never want to be humiliated again. Especially in front of the entire school. I don't really remember if Mum wrote me a note or not, but it didn't matter anyway. I got to school and told my sports teacher that I did not want to swim at the carnival as I was not feeling well. She said I shouldn't get out of swimming when she saw nothing wrong with me. I thought, well, I would do the best that I could, so I did not get into more trouble than I already had been in. It was time for our group to swim fifty meters freestyle. I thought it didn't seem that far, but I knew that I couldn't swim. I never wanted to get into the water after being in Uncle's dam. I just knew that everyone would laugh at me, and if it wasn't there because of the teachers, it would be after when no one was around.

The girls and I got on our blocks, and I was against some good swimmers. They got into their positions, leaning over, ready to jump in the water when the gun went off. They were already off and racing by the time I jumped into the pool. I struggled to swim. They were already at the end of the pool when I was halfway. I struggled to even make it to the end, but the whole school was waiting for me to finish. It seemed like forever until I got to the end. I was so embarrassed and humiliated in front of the whole school, and families were there too. I just wanted to get out and find somewhere to cry. I never wanted to cry in front of Uncle when I was hurting or upset, so I carried on letting people know that I didn't give a shit. But I did, it felt like being in the dam all over again; just a good laugh for everyone seeing this hopeless child who can't swim.

And that was fine because I should have been able to swim at my age; I just chose not to. Not long after that, I left school anyway. I felt that it was better for the teachers because this secret was killing me. The only way I knew how to release my pain was through my behavior. This was only going to get worse for me. I held it all inside and punished anyone that I could so that I could feel better myself. To this day, I still can't swim, but it is on my bucket list for this year. I have a great love for the ocean, and I love being around water, just not in it.

I remember another time when I was still living in Wallan, and my mum wanted you to throw me a party for my birthday at our house. I wasn't doing anything else that day as it was the weekend, and Mum was worried that I would find some way of drinking before my party. She sent me across the road to our friends Eddie and Pat. They lived in a railway house in Wallan East and had three boys. I knew Eddie would be drinking as it was the weekend, and he did not have to work. He always drank big, long-neck beers. Pat would give him his Bex powders to take, not sure what they were for, probably a headache or something like that. Ernie would open the packet of powder, put it in his mouth, and wash it down with his beer. He would always sneak me out of beer when Pat was not watching, and I would scull them down as quickly as I could to get some effect of his alcohol before I went home. When my friend came over to tell me to come home for my birthday party, I was drunk.

This was another time in my life when I just wanted to self-sabotage my night so everyone in the town would be right about me. I didn't remember the night and couldn't remember what Mum and my friends had bought me for my birthday. Alcohol was a better friend to me at this time of my life.

CHAPTER NINE
THE HARDEST WORK OF MY LIFE

Rehab and counselling were words I never thought would belong to me. I told myself for years that I wasn't "that bad," that I was just blowing off steam, that I could stop if I wanted to. But the truth was different. Alcohol had become my escape, my armour, and my mask. It was the silence I poured into a glass when the memories got too loud.

Walking into rehab stripped me of all the excuses. I couldn't pretend anymore. I had to face what I had been running from—my pain, my past, myself.

The truth is, addiction isn't just about the drinking. It's about the hurt that lives underneath it. Sitting in those rooms, talking to counsellors, listening to other broken voices, I began to understand that I wasn't drinking because I loved alcohol. I was drinking because I couldn't stand being me.

Counselling forced me to look at the girl I used to be—the child silenced by abuse, the teenager judged without anyone asking why, the woman who hid her pain behind laughter and swearing and another round of drinks. Piece by piece, I had to face her.

It was raw. It was ugly. There were days I wanted to quit, days when the craving felt bigger than me, when I thought drowning myself in alcohol again would be easier than feeling. But I kept showing up. I kept talking. I kept breaking open the walls I had built.

Through rehab and counselling, I began to hear a different voice—the one I thought had been lost forever. My own. A voice that told me I deserved to heal. That I wasn't what he did to me. That I didn't need to keep punishing myself. Recovery is not neat. It's not a straight line. It's a fight every day. But it was in those moments—sitting across from counsellors, crying in group rooms, choosing not to drink—that I began to live again.

Rehab didn't give me back the years I lost. But it gave me something even more important: the chance to choose the years ahead.

There was another time with Uncle when we were at Pop's house, and we would visit the cars, and I would sit in the front seat again with Uncle. We would play the same game with his penis, with him sitting in the car and pushing my face down on him to do things that he wanted me to do. I just didn't want to know what was happening. I loved pop; he was old, but he would always find time for me. I would sit next to him and just listen.

I remember on the days at home, when I was brushing my teeth and my gums started to bleed.

This happened for a while, and I was scared to tell Mum. I thought that there was something wrong with me. I was only fourteen at the time and was still going to school. Mum took me to a hospital dentist in Melbourne. The doctor told Mum that I had to have all my teeth taken out, and after my mouth had healed, they would replace them with dentures. I blamed myself. Was it because of Uncle or some of the things that he had done? I was booked to have some time off from school to have this procedure done.

Mum took me to the hospital in Melbourne. I stayed overnight and went home the next day. My gums were all sunken in, and I looked like an old lady. As a child, I never knew why this had happened to me. Dad wasn't there to explain it to me, and I don't think Mum really knew why this happened either.

I was at home and settled. The doctor had said that it was very important to keep rinsing my mouth with warm water. I always had a bucket next to me. I didn't want anyone touching my mouth or my face. I could do this all myself, I told Mum. I had been home for three weeks, and it was time for a visit to the hospital. When I went in with Mum to see the doctor, he told me to open my mouth to have a look at my gums and see how they were healing. He was disgusted with me for not taking care of my mouth.

Fuck off, I thought to myself. I don't care about my face or mouth or about having no teeth. I am just fine. I went home with Mum and couldn't get anything else done to get my dentures until I looked after my mouth properly. While I was at home, there was I boy I really liked; he lived in our area. He came around to Mum and Dad's house to visit me and wanted to take me for a drive. I didn't really care. I grabbed my bucket so I could have something to spit in. It was the first time that someone had seen me with no teeth. Slowly, I started to rinse my mouth out regularly, and my gums started to heal. Time to get impressions for my new teeth. Mum had said that they were going to cost a lot of money and that my dad wasn't very happy about it. I did feel it was my fault that I needed teeth. Eventually, I got my new teeth, and it was time to go back to school. I looked like Uncle's horse, Prince Opal; it took a long time for them to settle into my mouth. I didn't care about being teased as I felt different anyway.

Uncle had a friend who lived on our street. His name was Frank. He was heavily involved in the church, more than Uncle was, I think. He often donated a lot of his own money to the church. He had a big house just like Uncle's with a big verandah that was wrapped around the outside of it. This house also had a big combustion stove that smelled like burnt smoke when it had been on for a while.

Frank let people in the town use his land to keep their sheep, and they could keep the grass down. My friend asked me to go to Frank's as he had a big house, and he kept his sheep on his land. I said, "Okay." Little did I know that Frank was like Uncle, he liked to take his clothes off and play games with us. He would be naked and run around the house with his penis erect and have a big belly laugh, like it was so much fun.

Frank never hurt me like Uncle did. I just thought at the time that he liked to be naked around little girls. There was talk in the town that he may have been doing bad things to other people. I don't know if he was, but I never went back to his house again with my friend. In years to come, he had passed away and had left everything that he had at the church. Uncle had lots of friends; some I remember, some I don't. One day, Uncle and I went for a long drive, and he promised me that he would pay for me to have riding lessons. I was excited as my friend was a much better horse rider than me and I knew that I could get better. Uncle said I looked good sitting in the saddle on Prince Opal. He said that I looked like a natural. We went past Upper Plenty Road in the big property, with lots of land, and horses. I cannot remember exactly were.   Uncle and I got out of the car, I had my jodhpurs on and my riding boots, and my helmet. I thought I looked smart.

There was another man there with Uncle; he saddled up the horse that I was going to ride. I got some help from Uncle.   Uncle looked happy for a while. He grabbed the horse's reins and started walking the horse and then left it up to me to learn how to get it moving. I started to move slowly in the paddock. Then Uncle said that I wasn't sitting in the saddle right, and the horse could sense that I wasn't in control. He said it was enough for today, and we could go have a look around the property before we went home. There was a place we went to, and there was one other friend of Uncle's. I do not remember that day, and I do not really care if I ever do. At times, when I was afraid of Uncle, somehow my brain could just block out bad things. I was paralyzed by my fear of Uncle.

When we went back home, Auntie was doing her washing. She had this big steel, long wire ropes out in their backyard on their land; the stable was out there, too. Auntie was so fussy about hanging out her clothes. I used to laugh and think to myself, this stuff shouldn't be that hard. Everything was hung from the largest to the smallest. Auntie said there was nothing better than putting the washing on the line outside on a breezy day to dry. When everything was dry, she would go out with her basket, take everything off one by one, fold them neatly, then put them in the basket and take them inside.

When my husband and I were living on the street up from their home, if she was taking a walk down to the general store, and saw that we weren't home, she would go out the back of our house and take all our washing off the line and leave it in on our verandah, so it was nice and dry. She always thought of others. There was a time when I was older that Uncle wanted to take Auntie back to Tasmania to see her family.

He wanted me to come with him and Auntie, but Auntie was getting angry with me. She was getting jealous of all the time Uncle was spending with me. We were standing out front of Uncle and Auntie's house, talking about Tasmania. Uncle was cuddling and kissing me. Auntie went crazy, for the first time in my childhood, she had had enough of Uncle. She told me to piss off home and not to come back and told Uncle that I wasn't coming to Tasmania with them. I started to cry, ran across the road, and thought to myself Why does Auntie hate me so much In this moment, it's Uncle that's the monster, not me.

I didn't go to Tasmania, but I went to summer camp with my school, Broadford High. I think it was at the Grampians. We all slept in a camp place that had dorms with lots of bunk beds.

I was pretty screwed up. I wanted to get away from Wallan, and in other ways, I didn't. My friends were so excited to start all their camp activities. I was afraid I might have to get undressed in front of

People, especially when showering or swimming. I was embarrassed by my body. I could see on the outside what Uncle had been doing to me, but no one else saw me this way. I had a lady teacher; I think her name was Miss Coppinger. I needed to try to get out of group activities, but we had only been away for two days. I just didn't know why I said yes to going. I decided to get out of everything. I would just say that I was sick, and we did go for a hike that day in the bush. The fresh air was crisp, the rocks were hard to walk on, and everything was just so green and breathtaking. For a while, I had forgotten about Uncle. I knew that my teacher was kind and caring and so good to us kids. I just wasn't used to healthy attention. I thought that everyone was going to hurt me in some way. I ended up feeling sick, and my teacher just about carried me all the way back to camp.

When we got back to camp, I lay on the top bunk bed. The other kids were sitting near the teacher. I heard her say that they were going somewhere else when I went to sleep.

I felt at the camp that I no longer had to be on high alert, and I started to enjoy my time there. The whole time I was being abused by my uncle in my mind, I never knew how to say no to people. I lost my voice when I was five. It didn't matter to me if I was hurting as long as no one else was. If we went out and my husband behaved like an arsehole, I would feel like I had behaved like that, and it wasn't me. I don't like to see anyone hurting in my family, as I feel like I have done something wrong to cause it. With Uncle, I always had to do something more and something better, and then it was never okay. At times, he would say that I was a good girl, but the dark times remain.

The first time I went to a mental health rehab center was in Western Australia. It was a public one in Perth for alcohol abuse. I had been struggling with this on and off since I was fifteen.

I had never confronted this before; it was daunting, but I was up for it.

They monitored you while you were coming out of alcohol. When I got home, it wasn't long before I started to drink again. It was quite a while after this that I was living in Queensland, and the court case with Uncle was over. I had been going through therapy with Victims of Crime while the court case was ongoing. At this stage, my doctor in Buderim had talked about a stint in a private mental health hospital and had said that Victims of Crime had requested it if I wanted to go.

There were several therapists that you could see there while in treatment, and you got to stay in your own room. I was heavily addicted to Benzos and had been using them throughout Uncle's trial.

This was my way of being completely numb, but now, I had to come off them and find a healthy way to live. The first week, I still got to take my benzos so they could start to wean me off them. I was as high as a kite, bloody great, I thought. During the day, we had a group meeting for anxiety and depression, ways of coping without drugs or alcohol. You didn't have to go if you didn't want to, but I went most times unless I had my own private counselling session. I met so many people who were happy to share their stories with me. They had a smokers' corner out the front of the hospital. I didn't smoke, but I went out there every day to listen to how everyone was doing. The first few nights were tough, coming off so many pills coming off. I was pressing the buttons for the nurses on the night shift to come into my room. I was hallucinating, thinking that people were climbing up the trees outside my room to break in. What a laugh the nurses must have had; they would tell me that there was no one in my room. I didn't believe them; this was real to me. It got a little easier after the first week; at least I wasn't seeing invisible people anymore. When I was down to just taking a few tablets a day, I was feeling great, not as out of it. I was able to have a day's leave and spend some time out of the hospital. I had never realized that being addicted to prescription drugs would be so hard to come off for me. When I finally got home, when I couldn't sleep and just wanted some Valium temazepam, I thought about rehab and the person that people saw in me when I first got there. It's been fourteen years, and I have never taken one since.

There was a lady whom I had been put in touch with through Victims of Crime. She lived in Melbourne. She knew so much about child historical abuse; she was good to talk to.

I had been speaking to her for a few years. I shared my story about wanting to write a book. She said, "Why not?" "I have written one for someone else. Send what you have got to me, and I will help you to achieve this.

I had been sending her my work for about two years after the court hearing. Every time I thought of things, I would write them down and send them to her. Over time, I must have sent a lot of information to her to process for me. She never really talked about it much when we were together. Then one day she said that she had a confession to make, not knowing what she was about to say. She told me that everything that I had sent her was still in the envelopes and that she hadn't been doing my book.

She offered to send it back, and I agreed. It really didn't matter; you don't really have a way of deleting your mind, or shit would be so much easier to deal with in life.

From day one, with making my statement to the police officer and having all the services available to me from Victims of Crime, I was able to learn all about why I had so many distorted beliefs, not only with life but within myself. Every time I think that I shouldn't go for that job or take on something that I never thought I could do, I go for it anyway. The most challenging thing for me growing up after leaving Wallan was my lack of education. I was okay just being a mum and anything else out of that circle to feel more worthy, but I was too frightened to face.

Finally, I thought that I would try going back to school; in my head, I thought that I was dumb and would probably be laughed at. But all I wanted growing up was to become a schoolteacher or an air hostess. I enrolled in a TAFE course first; it was Cert III in community services. I enjoyed the mental health modules and being around people.

I told myself that I was worthy, and I was going to give it my best shot. I told the group in my course that I was a high school dropout. And that was the truth, so I had a lot of learning to do. I wasn't the only one nervous; there were many who felt the same as me. I just needed confidence in myself. I completed my Cert III and got enough confidence to go on to do my Diploma in Community Service.

This was always what I wanted to do, and now I was saying to myself, "Fuck you, Uncle, I am not stupid." I graduated from my diploma to learn about people like Uncle, who groom you when you are so young, you really don't stand a chance when someone has that power over you.

My sister and I talk about Uncle at times, and we both deal with it in different ways. She was more of a homebody, staying in her room as a child and teenager, as that is where she felt the safest.

I, on the other hand, just went on pretending that this never had an impact on me. I could just suck it up and put on my mask for the day.

At night, the visions of Uncle would remain in my head. I always wanted the door open when we were sleeping; there had to be a light on somewhere in the house.

I closed my eyes every time my husband and I were intermate. I was used to doing this with Uncle. It seemed to be just what my body wanted me to do; it felt safe not to see what was happening. Uncle forced himself on me and made me do horrible things so that he would be happy. That's what sex meant to me at sixteen: do as you are told if you want someone to like you, or they won't want you.

I only wish that I could have liked myself enough to know what I wanted for my future. Instead, my brain taught me how to survive, and nothing else mattered to me.

I don't remember growing up with my sister or much of my brother until I was older and had left home. I don't remember playing together or even fighting; sis has more of a memory in that area than me.

I don't remember having a bond with any of my brothers when Uncle was abusing us.

I think at times it is better to remember trauma because, without it, for me, there is no me. She still exists where I am all tangled up like a web.

I had a picture of my sister and me when she was around five or six, and I was around twelve or thirteen. My sister said when we were picking out some pictures for the book, "Look at you in that picture, sis, you have sad eyes."

In this photo, I didn't see myself as Susan, the little girl from this small country town. She was gone, invisible to me to see. I felt that, emotionally, my growth had stopped. I grew taller and developed physically, but mentally and physically, I had shut down.

THE VISION THAT REMAINS IN MY DREAMS FROM THE MONSTER, THE WOLF OF WALLAN.

Some nights, I would wake up feeling like someone had hit me, and it came from out of nowhere. An unexpected punch. That moment in my dream felt like I was re-living a moment from Uncle. A memory of being hurt when I wasn't expecting it. When I woke from this dream, I felt that this had really happened again.

When I would realize that I was in my own home and safe, I was so relieved, I would say to myself It's only a dream, Susan, it's okay, flip the switch and start your day with good vibes; it's just the past, not the present.

Another dream that I had about Uncle is that I felt that I could never escape. I would dream about cutting my way out of places with knives and removing anything that was on my way to escape.

In my dreams, there would be furniture that I had to move to get closer to getting away.

But everything that I pushed through to escape, there was no end to this; it just kept on going, there were more barriers to break. I felt trapped, then I would wake up and go, "What the hell was that all about?"

A few things would come to my mind. Was I trying to run away from myself, or was it Uncle I needed to escape from?

I have a dream about a big padlock, and Uncle must open it; he has lots of keys, and I know when I get there, I can't get out.

I never really knew who or what person was living in my head at one time.

My hometown of Wallan used to feel so safe; it was free to enjoy such a tight-knit community, and to be very trusting of everyone, especially Uncle and Auntie. I never really understood why I was drawn to keep going over there. Apart from my love of Auntie, before I knew it, I was completely groomed by Uncle.

The fear of hurting my Auntie in this town if I told my secret and not knowing if Uncle would carry through with all his threats that he was going to do to me and my family.

I just became a lost child, lost in my abuse at the hands of Uncle, and I was frightened to use my voice. The drives I took with Uncle as a child in the country town of Wallan were at times just dirt roads, Uncle's car would get all dusty if it was a windy day, and if you put the windows down, the dust would blow in my face. This was mainly the back roads where we would go through to get to some of Uncle's friends' houses. Some drives were pretty; the paddocks were dry; they had hay bales all over them to feed the cows. Some of the houses had big, long driveways, and the house would be in the middle of the big paddocks.

Growing up with Uncle, I learned that if I was upset or hurt about something that Uncle did to me and I wanted him to stop, I needed to find a place to hide those feelings. So, as I got older and was in a relationship, when I felt that I should have said something and stuck up for myself, I never did. I just felt that I didn't matter and that I would rather just suck it up and be quiet, just like I was conditioned to do with Uncle.

Even if I knew the answer to questions on the TV or the games that we would play, I would never say things out loud for fear of being laughed at.

Going back to school gave me a voice and the confidence to know that I can do what I want, if I really want it.

There was another time when I was still at Broadford High School, and our class was having a blue light disco in Kilmore. I really love to dance and listen to music. I could get so lost in the music that I didn't

Think about Uncle. I felt safe, and some teachers from the school were there to supervise in case the kids smuggled in alcohol.

I was so busy dancing that I didn't care about what the girls were doing in the toilets.

I was having so much fun; my hair was wet, and I was sweating. I was behaving like I had been drinking, but I wasn't. I knew of a few who were. One of the teachers came up to me and accused me of drinking. She said she was so disappointed in me, and I had to go home. Everyone thought that I was rebellious, a bad kid. And, yet again, I wished that I had dared to tell someone.

At the end of my school days at Broadford High, I basically spent lunch time and recesses sitting on my own, normally on the portable class steps. I had never felt so alone. I wanted so much to be out playing with my friends, laughing, and enjoying being a teenager. The secret that I had been keeping was too heavy for me, and school wasn't an option for me anymore. I would drink to numb the pain.

When I was at Uncle's house, most of the time, if Auntie was home, he wouldn't be in the house much. He always seemed to be doing something out in the paddocks. Auntie would often stand at her big window and look across the road to Uncle's sister's place. She would say that she was a troublemaker. My dad had a strong relationship with Uncle's sister. He would spend hours over at her place having cups of tea and talking. My dad never spoke badly about Uncle's sister; he did say a lot about Uncle only when he wasn't around. One day, we were sitting around Auntie's table for some tea and her homemade cupcakes, with jelly and cream on the tops of them. They were always one of my favorites. The kitchen was next to a window, and there hung a white lace curtain on it. It fell to the end of the window. It really didn't look that white, like it needed a wash. Sometimes we girls would do things for Uncle, like drawing cards telling him how much we cared about him, or it would be badges that we had earned at Brownies or Scouts. I think this was another way for Uncle to groom us.

At times, I wondered if Uncle loved Auntie, because every time I was there, he would always tell her to piss off somewhere.

When we girls got together to make our statements and speak up about Uncle, people in the town started talking. Some have suspected all along about Uncle is abusing young children in the town.

There would be whispers and gossip, but never anything else. When I was with Uncle, I knew nothing about sex. I thought that I was just making him happy. He had a way of making it okay, and he was always nice to me later. As I got older, Uncle made my vagina feel funny all the time.

There are times when I would have flashbacks, like when I was out somewhere, and a man would have the same cologne that Uncle wore. They would be talking and tilting their neck to the side, with their hand up against their chin. They would be wearing smart dress pants pulled up past their belly. And they would have that stupid laugh. This would remind me of the times he would be in those types of clothing with his big belly around his pants. And we would often be sitting in his car or one of Pop's properties, then the zip would come down, he would pull his penis out, and ask me to play with it, push my head down on it until we went home. When Uncle and I went to his workplace in Kilmore, we would always go into his office. We would normally go on a Saturday, I think people worked there in the morning, but they had left by the afternoon.

Uncle was the boss, so he always had access to different places.

When our family was together, Uncle would put on a good show. He would be kind to my sister and me, and very careful about where he went and the time that he was away.

There were times when he would still take a chance by bathing my sister, before she went home, while Mum and Dad were still in the house.

Sometimes when we were out at a party in the town, he would go missing for a while. My brother found him once. He was inside talking to the children.

Uncle knew how to groom children so he could satisfy his needs; he was a master manipulator. He had fooled the whole town.

I remember as I grew older, I never wanted my photo taken. If I had seen pictures of myself, I would hate them. I was the only one who hated myself and could see the pain that I had been hiding through my eyes. No one else could imagine the self-hatred that I carried around for years.

I wish that I had taken more photos of my family together, but I was always happy to be the one behind the camera, not in front of it. I have so many pictures of my husband and our two children. There wasn't enough time taken for our whole family together because of how much I couldn't stand to look at myself. I remember when I flew home from Perth to make my statement about Uncle. I stayed at my girlfriend's house in Whittlesea, Victoria. I said that I was going to take a brown paper bag with me, just in case I found

It's hard to breathe. Breathing into a bag always seemed to slow my breathing down a little, and that lump in my throat that was blocking the airway seemed to move a little and let me breathe.

I was speaking to Sergeant Julie Trimble from the sexual abuse team at Seymore police station. She had come to Wallan police station that day to take my statement.

I was shaking and was petrified to say what I needed to say.

I had a few moments where I needed to breathe in the brown paper bag, but I was so happy to have said what I needed to say about Uncle. For the first time since I was a little girl, someone was making this monster accountable for what he had done.

I would have these dreams about being in the courtroom when they charged Uncle with repeated historical child sexual abuse. And for all the girls, he was never going to be released from jail. I would be filled with so much joy, then wonder how he would feel if someone punched him when he was unaware. Or wanted to fiddle with him without permission. But that was just in my dreams, and I would never want anyone to be hurt the way Uncle hurt my sister and me. Seeing him in jail for just a few days would have been enough for me.

Everywhere I moved in my life, it seemed like Uncle moved with me. I carried self-hatred about myself, as well as the blame and shame. It seemed to never be Uncle's fault, as I always found ways to blame myself.

I think that I just created stuff in my head that I believed. This would always be a distortion.

No matter how many times people tell you that you are a good person, there is always a belief that they are just saying that to be nice.

I don't know how many times Uncle told me I was his princess and his favorite little girl. I think that he said that because in the beginning, I never resisted what he wanted me to do.

The times in Uncle's house, down in the back room where his boys slept, the single beds with the brown bedspreads, were some of the times when I just wanted to forget, put it somewhere in my brain, and forget about it to just survive.

There were things that I didn't talk about in my statement to Julie, things I was so ashamed of. It wasn't my shame to carry; it was Uncle's.

Whenever I move around the state with my family or travel overseas, it's like I pack two suitcases. One with my clothes and essentials for our trip. And the other was packed away with

Self-hatred, blame, shame, and a distorted body image of myself. Something that travelled with me everywhere that I went. I was a different person at home than I was in public and around people, especially family.

I don't understand why I felt the need to be liked so much; maybe because I had to pretend to be someone else to purely survive what happened to me.

If there was something bad had happened in my life, I would always feel bad and say to myself that, maybe, it was just because I let Uncle do bad things to me. So, I am being punished for it. It's bloody ridiculous.

I don't think now that I am a bad person. I was just in the wrong place at the wrong time. Who knew that there was an evil monster living in the town that my mum and dad decided to move to?

Uncle used physical violence to get his way, and he was relentless in his prey. Becoming withdrawn from life was something I felt safe about.

Misusing substances was my way of coping with depression. I had nightmares about Uncle in the stable at the back of their home. At times, I just wanted to punish myself or hurt myself, as then the pain would go away for a while.

I often talk about being a little girl when I was with Uncle, but I abandoned her growing up because I had to. In my mind, that abused and broken girl didn't exist. I just carried on as a teenager and never wanted any memory of my childhood.

This worked for a while until I started to wonder about what movie was my favorite. What did I enjoy the most about Mum and Dad? Did I ever have a relationship with my brothers?

This went on and on, but at times when I tried to block Uncle out, I blocked the good times out as well.

I often wondered if Uncle only fostered girls because Auntie was such a beautiful person, and they would gel with her easily. Then Uncle could spoil them with sweets and lollies, tell them how sweet they were, and then the wolf of Wallan could strike again and get his sexual needs met. Sick bastard.

Later, when our daughter was born, we were getting her christened in a church in Kilmore, and Auntie and Uncle were attending that day. I never wanted him there; I just wanted Auntie. He stood at the front with the priests, trying to sell his perfect family image of a respectful, kind man. One of them was a very dear friend whom I had seen when horse riding in his group of friends.

He made me feel sick to my stomach. How many little girls had he preyed on and stolen their innocence? There must have been hundreds over his lifetime. Little did I know at the time when you were sexually abusing me, he was abusing my sister, who was only four at the time. My girlfriend from school, Carly, is another girl whom we knew about, but didn't want to press charges. And there is a lot more that I can't mention in this book, as they don't want to relive the pain and heartache of what was done to them.

Uncle had no boundaries in his abuse, whether he knew the parents of the children in this town or not. There was no remorse; his sexual drive was endless.

CHAPTER TEN
LEARNING TO LIVE WITHOUT NUMBING

*L*eaving rehab didn't mean life was suddenly easy. It meant facing the world without my old shield. No more hiding behind alcohol. No more quick escape when the past pressed in. I had to live wide open, raw, and sober.

At first, it felt unbearable. Every feeling I had run from came flooding back. Fear, shame, grief. Nights stretched on forever. I couldn't switch them off with a drink anymore. The silence was loud, and I had to sit inside it.

Counselling kept me from drowning. Week after week, I sat in that chair and forced myself to be honest. I spoke about my childhood, about the man who stole it, about the years I buried it all under alcohol. My counsellor never flinched. She let me fall apart in that room, and then reminded me that I could put myself back together.

I began to see patterns—how the abuse had trained me to hate myself, how the bottle had become another form of punishment. Slowly, I started to believe I didn't have to keep carrying his voice in my head.

There were still days I wanted to run. Days when it felt too much, when my skin crawled with old memories. But each time I stayed sober, each time I let myself feel instead of numb, I found a new piece of strength.

I learned to sit with pain without trying to escape it. I learned to speak out loud what I once thought would kill me if I ever admitted it. And in those moments, a small light began to grow.

Recovery wasn't about becoming perfect. It was about becoming real. For the first time in years, I was beginning to live as myself—not as the broken girl, not as the woman with the mask, but as Susan.

I did felt safe when I first moved into this town, living as a normal little girl, climbing trees with my friend. Catching tadpoles and bugs in the water, riding my bike. Driving cars when I was barely old enough to drive. The freedom that I felt was endless; if I got home before it was dark, there were basically no rules.

I loved the smell of the country air, and I also loved it when it poured with rain. My only downfall in this small town of Wallan was that Uncle was living there. Tucked away at the end of the street, waiting for his next prey. I often wondered if he ever thought about what he had done to many young children and how it was wrong. How would we live our lives as adults? Would we ever learn to trust anyone again?

Would we automatically feel pleasure sexually if someone did the same thing to us in our adult relationship that he did to us as little girls?

He certainly spent his entire life as a Jekyll and Hyde; he always had a plan.

I can't imagine how he felt when he learned he and Auntie were accepted as foster parents and could pick and choose who to take in and look after.

The pool of victims was growing, and Uncle's secret was safe from everyone living in and around our town. I think back now and think of all the places that he took to us girls, it being a small country town with lots of dirt roads, parking bays, and lots of places on his property. With Auntie knowing to never come and bother him.

I think when we went over to Pops and his brother and sister's place, he knew he was safe, and she would never question him. And Auntie thought he used to spend hours talking over there. But no, it was half-talk, then walking to the back shed for his sexual pleasure before going home. I never thought that his double life would take him into his eighties; he should have been the one to get sick, not Auntie.

I never liked any affection in my world as I grew up. Because it was forced on me by The Wolf of Wall Street.

I don't like anyone who gets too close to me, as in my mind, I think that they will eventually hate me anyway.

I loved Auntie in such a different way; never in her life was she ever cruel to me.

I never really knew where I stood with Uncle, whether he would be the nice one or the evil monster, who needed to fulfill his sexual needs.

I never felt comfortable undressing for activities at school or ever undressing in front of anyone. I just would say that I was not getting undressed, and I would go into the toilet and get changed. Then I get teased by my school friends for being embarrassed. I hated my body. I never wanted to bring any attention to myself. I remember being in an English class at Broadford High School, where we were all having turns of reading a book out to the class. I was shaking, I said to myself, "Please, please do not ask me."

Everyone was going to laugh at me. I wasn't a confident person. Uncle would laugh at me and sometimes embarrass me in front of people. I eventually had to get up, and because I was already panicking and anxious, I sounded like I was still in primary school, even though I knew how to read.

I just think that toward the end of year ten in school, I wanted to get into trouble for attention. It wasn't the real me. But I seemed to only get attention now when I would behave badly. Uncle's secret was too heavy for me to carry.

So, when I left school for a while, I created someone who just wasn't me. I never wanted to have an opinion. This did not matter to me. I would be quiet if we were sitting around a fire talking about the world. I never thought that my voice mattered. I would be so embarrassed if I tried to answer a question, and it was so stupid. I think my husband would feel embarrassed for me.

No one knew when I was young how much pain I had been holding in. And that's what I wanted it to be like. I used to think that if I told people that they would think that I had done something to Uncle to make him do things for me.

They would want to know what I did and why I did not stop him. I blamed myself.

I used to believe it was because I wore dresses, and Uncle said that I always looked so pretty in them. When he asked me to come and sit on his knee, I should not have sat in the middle of his legs. I would use any excuse to blame myself.

As I got older, I realized that it was never my fault, but it took years to lose the shame and guilt that I forever carry every day.

It seemed to me that I had built a brick wall in my head. The shame, guilt, and blame. They need to say no to opportunities to educate oneself or being offered a great job.

I would self-sabotage myself before I would even get the chance to have an interview.

I knew that I could do the job, but I was never confident enough to get through the interview.

Before I went for the job, I would tell myself that I was not good enough, and I did not know why they even wanted to see me.

This was okay for me now because I loved being a mum, so I stayed in my comfort zone where the only person who judged me was myself. At times, it was like Uncle was living in my mind with me. It was Uncle's constant voice repeatedly in my head. I had to learn to switch from the past to the present.

Many times, I would pretend that I was on the beach, the sea looked so peaceful, and the waves went wherever they wanted to go.

I would think about how I am still here and that I was able to meet someone, get married, and have children.

Something to be grateful for; at times, this did work, and I would drift off to sleep.

I thought that as I got older, I would try different ways to cope without alcohol and prescription drugs.

In my therapy today, my therapist asked me a question. "What would be your perfect morning to wake up to?" I said I didn't know. I don't have any idea; I have never really thought about it.

"What do you enjoy when you are feeling happy?"

I thought for a minute. Waking up in a cabin in the woods, with an open burning wood fire.

Outside would have been a wet day, pouring with rain, maybe hailstones as well.

I would be snuggled near the fire, sitting near the window, looking outside, and loving the sound of the rain. Not far from the cabin would be a creek with the water rushing quickly over the rocks.

Then, not far away again, would be the beach. I could sit there watching the waves smashing back and forth on the rocks. The water is so free; here, there is no judgment of anyone's soul. The beach is a place where I would like to rest when I pass. I feel alive when I sit looking at the ocean.

I loved to ride Missy and Prince Opal. Missy was the first, then Prince Opal.

I did pick out Prince Opal because he had a white diamond on his face; he was a light brown color. Uncle knew that I was in love with him, and this would keep me going over this house and spending more time with him in the stable.

There were times when Uncle would not worry about getting Missy or Prince Opal ready for me to ride when we were in his shed out in the backyard.

As he had other things on his mind. He would say "Clean up the shed a little, make Missy some food with hay, bits of straw, and brown Yukie molasses that smelled so bad. It was so strong, at times I would hold my nose to avoid the smell.

Uncle did have a lot of bits and pieces in his shed. Sometimes he would act like he was my doctor and spread my legs to look at my vagina and do things with it. This is one memory.

Uncle was standing very close to me while I was on the bench with my legs open, and uncle was putting things in me. He said that it was ok, he was just looking to make sure that I was ok. He could make me feel nice again, like all the other times he did.

I am in my sixties now, and I always wondered why I cannot get Uncle out of my skin and body. I have had years of therapy on and off.

Yet, I still have not been able to let my adult life connect with my inner child, so we can become one, as she is safe now, and I can be the person who can protect her.

I think that all along, by not allowing myself to think of my childhood, I pretended not to have ever had one.

I figured that the only way to heal is to allow myself to grieve for the loss of my childhood. The child that I decided to lay rest at the hands of Uncle.

This, to my mind, was the only way to protect myself so that I could live on and survive growing older.

In my latest therapy session, I talked a little about forgiveness and why I cannot get in touch with that little girl and forgive her; she did nothing wrong to deserve what Uncle did to her. I have forever struggled with my body image and what I believed people would see me as.

I thought people would see me as Uncle did: weak, vulnerable, and easy to take advantage of. But from Uncle, I learned not to have a voice. I would say things to him, like he is hurting me, and to please stop. I did not like what he was doing to me.   His grip on me after speaking would put the fear of God in me, and I would say to myself to stay calm, do not resist, or I would get hurt.

t used to feel nice as a child, having other people in your life like your mum and dad, people to feel safe around. People, your parents trusted you in places when they could not make it. There was never a question about a child's safety in a small country town.

I used to feel so embarrassed when I had to get undressed in front of people, even when I went to the doctor. My blood pressure would be through the roof when I get to see the doctor. He said that I probably had white coat syndrome, the stress of not knowing what was going to happen. It happens to a lot of people. My question would be, is he going to ask me to take my clothes off? I just never felt like I could trust anyone, especially men.

I hated anyone touching or rubbing my breasts; my body would just shut down. It didn't feel nice. It reminded me of Uncle's big hands rubbing repeatedly my breasts when I was five. I never had breasts, but he would make my nipples hard. I hate that to this day.

There are still things today that trigger me.   I think that sex is going to lead to something that I cannot control. The fear of being in that moment and vulnerable never leaves me.

Somehow, I am always on high alert. Never really felt free to explore the freedom of a healthy sexual relationship.

I never cared if I was being pleased sexually, because it was always about pleasing Uncle when I was a little girl. I continued in my adulthood to just not to give a shit. It meant nothing to me.

If I thought about how different I would want my life to be now, it would have been to let all my walls down. Take the protection that I built around myself down, and do not be afraid to live outside the box that I had created for myself.

Tell people how you feel, whether it is good or bad, value yourself, feel your fear, and do what you want to.

Don't give a shit about judgment, and who is going to judge you anyway, as they sure will anyway. If I say that I am on antidepressants, people will have their views. Do what suits you.

In my world, I was so sick of doing what was expected of me; I was just a people pleaser, a learned behavior from my childhood.

I found that even making my statement about Uncle to the police officer. I could never get the words out of my mouth as to what I wanted and needed to say.

I wanted to say all what Uncle did to me, but I was so ashamed of myself. I was still at this stage, believing that no one could believe what Uncle was capable of.

I think of that one night, the big padlock hanging from the gate. It was always frightening, as I think I knew what that meant when Uncle would open it. Then make sure it was locked again before he continued to go farther inside. He had to make sure that no one would find us. They were never going to, as he was the only one who had the keys.

I have flashbacks on how big the fence looked to me, as I was only small; to me, it looked like prison gates. And the fact is that through my therapy, I always talked about feeling like everything within my trauma was heavily locked away in a prison cell in my head.

Uncle did a really bad thing that evening after I rang my mum. I sat on the office chair, and one of the phones was on the office desk. I remember my uncle starting to play with me. I do not really remember how my clothes were taken off. But uncle was lying on top of me, and this time he did not get off for what seemed to be longer than the times before when we were there.

He was moving up and down and pushing his penis inside me, he was rubbing my breasts, moving his hands up and down, and squeezing my nipples tight.

I was paralyzed with fear, so I thought to myself, I don't care I just lay there like a rag doll.

When you are satisfied, I don't know how my clothes got on, whether I put them on or my uncle did. But it was dark, and I had to go home. Uncle walked me out and locked the Gate behind him. He watched me run across the road to Mum and Dad's house. Then he went home inside to Auntie'

I felt so numb when I went home. I wanted to boil the kettle and pour it over my skin. I wanted my mind to concentrate on my burn and not uncle.

I wanted to hide the pain that I was feeling inside of me, so then, when horrible behavior would surface, just another day, another mask.

CHAPTER ELEVEN

I keep thinking that when I die, it will be from suffocation or choking to death.

When I am in the situation of choking on my food, or something gets caught in my throat, it takes my mind back to the dam with Uncle, and I start to freak out. I think that I am going to die. My husband just thinks that I overreact and that just get a grip on myself, that I am not going to die.

But to me, I am five years old, I am back in the dam on Uncle's property, I am choking, swallowing dam water, trying to save myself. Uncle thought trying to save myself was somehow very funny.

The trauma of that day is a demon that I still need to hunt down and deal with

I still can't swim to this day, but I can still do the dog paddle to save myself. Like I did that day when Uncle threw me into the dam and tried to drown me. I think again that he got off on seeing me beg for help.

This always put fear on me and made him more controlling and powerful in my eyes, so the next time he wanted to be pleased, I would not dare resist. Same as in the paddock when I was riding Missy. He punched me in the face deliberately. He meant it. I was only between twelve and thirteen. It was only when my nose started to bleed that he said that he was sorry. Bullshit.

When I fell off Missy that day, Uncle did not tighten her saddle properly; he knew if he gave her a good hit on her flanks that I was stuffed. He laughed, enjoying every moment of my humiliation.

My survival for him was to black out at times and pretend that this just was not happening. I trained my mind not to feel anything at the times that he was doing things to me. I would simply pretend that he was the nice Uncle, not the bad one.

I remember another day when I went over to Uncle's house to see him and Auntie. It was another cold and rainy day. I just loved the wet and rainy days in the country, and I always knew that their house would be warm. It would have that burnt smell that I loved. The heater would be on in the front room, and if Auntie was home, I would get something yummy to eat.

When Uncle took me into his bedroom, where he and Auntie slept, I thought it was a pretty room. The bed was big, and I remember it being a little high up from the ground. I thought that if I fell, I could really hurt myself. Auntie had this dressing table in their room. It was dark wood, like antique furniture. On Auntie's dressing table, she had an oval mirror that stood on top of their dresser. Auntie loved to brush my hair; she said that I was like the girl that she never had. I did think that she loved me.

When Auntie finishes doing my hair, I grab the brush from the dressing table and pretend to be a singer. I would hold it to my lips and sing.

She would laugh at me and tell me she did not think I'd ever be a singer. We both would laugh. I was sitting in the lounge one day warmly, and Uncle said to go into Auntie's room. I don't really remember what his reason for this was.

He started to undress me, then lay me on the big bed, it was nice and warm in there. I was looking at Auntie's pretty mirror, then Uncle started to take his clothes off. He would always play with my breasts first; I think that he did like feeling my nipples. He would lie on top of me, put his penis between my legs, and move himself all around my body. Then ask me if I felt that fuzzy feeling again between my legs, and that if I did, I was a good girl. I made him happy again. And it was time to go to the kitchen and get some sweets and a milkshake. I did love the way that Uncle made my milkshake.

I would sit at the table in the kitchen table near Auntie's lace curtains that looked out into their sunroom. I would ask Uncle about some of the things pinned up on Auntie's curtains.

They were scout badges of little girls that he knew. They gave them to him because they wanted him to be proud of them. Almost like a trophy for him to remember how many girls he had been molesting.

There was one badge that I did not recognize. I had a bad feeling that this person was someone who had lived close by.

My little sister was part of the Scouts and Brownies club that Uncle took her to, as well as some other girls. She said that going with Uncle to the Scouts was one of the worst times in her life.

Uncle knew other men he was involved with, who were doing the same thing to little girls as he was in Wallan. I do remember some places we went to where Uncle was doing things to me, and his friend was doing naughty stuff too.

When Auntie and I were in the kitchen on our own, we would sit at the table many times with Auntie's China cup and tea saucers, sipping tea.

Aunties would always get up to check on the stove to make sure that it had enough wood. She would give the stove a shove with the poker stick, and the buts of fireballs would come out of the stove.

She would look out of her big window that looked straight into Pop's house and say the same thing that she would say repeatedly: "Uncle's sister is a witch of a thing, just a troublemaker trying to stir things up all the time."

But she never stopped him from going over to see them, as this was a safe place for Uncle to take me back home to Auntie's house through Pop's backyard, so that he could have another go at me.

When my little sister was over at my uncles at different times, there was always a time when we would need to have a bath. Most of the time would be if we had been in the stable with uncle, or just getting dirty playing in the yard or the paddocks.

Uncle and aunties' bath wasn't a big area, but it was long, and I think that the bath was alongside one of the walls.

You would always tell Auntie that you were just going to check on me when I was already in the bath, or you were undressing to get me ready for a bath.

I knew what that would mean, you would get the soap was my breasts, then follow down my tummy, rubbing the soap all over me. Then go down to my vagina to wash me all clean, you would say to me.

You would tell me to open my legs, just put one leg on one side of the bath and the other on the other side. Then I can make you really clean for when you go home to your mum and das house.

Do I get some lollies or a milkshake when I go out, uncle? That depends on you, darling. Are you going to be a good girl?

Yes, Uncle, you will be happy with me then, I will still be your favorite.

Auntie had a good friend, Katie; they would go for long walks around the roads in Wallan East. The roads at the back of Uncle's house were still dirty. Both Auntie and Katie would, at times, be out for a few hours at a time. I think Katie was one of Auntie's true friends. Sometimes Uncle would go over to Katie's house with Auntie. I would hope that there were not any little girls visiting, or maybe Katie's grandchildren. Especially if they were young girls.

I think that at the times when Uncle was confronted with abusing my little sister, Kate had always had her suspicions about Uncle. She had heard the way Uncle would talk to me and always give me lots of attention, more than he ever gave Auntie when she often visited Uncle and Auntie's house. When Auntie plans a shopping day together, they would normally be out for the entire day.

Auntie never had her license to drive a car, so she always relied on Uncle to take her places that she could not get to. But Auntie loved going to the big shopping centers for the day with Kate, as Wallan never had one at that time.

They would always plan the day that they were going to head into town. Auntie would put this on her calendar to make sure that Uncle knew where she was going.

This would leave Uncle free for the day to plan his next move. If he saw Auntie was going out with Katie, Uncle would arrange something with me. Or I would be just visiting Auntie before Katie came around to pick her up and take her out.

On some of these days, Uncle and I would either go for a drive, or we would do things, and I would get lollies and a milkshake. Then I would go home, sometimes it would be my little girlfriend that were both over there at the same time together fighting for Uncle's attention.

At the time we were both there together, I never knew what Uncle was doing to her. And she never knew what he was doing to me. It was only years later that we discovered the same things were happening to both of us and my little sister.

There was a time that Uncle took the two of us for a drive to one of his favorite parking bays on top of Pretty Sally Hill, called now Hidden Valley.

I was with Uncle; we were sitting together; he asked me to sit close to him. When we go for drives, he likes it when I sat close to him.

My friend was sitting in the back seat, and we never knew that Uncle was doing the same thing to both of us that day. When he finished with me, my friend would sit in front of me, and Uncle would be playing with her. Uncle was insatiable when it came to abusing young girls. He was always wanting more. He was never satisfied like a wolf. Uncle was hungry for power and his next prey. Even when he knew that his victim was resisting, he would use his power and strength to make ensure that his needs are met.

There was a place Uncle took me for a drive one night, on Darraweit Guim Road, where there was a turn off the road somewhere. My mum used to work at the chock farm there when I was young. This one night, it was cold when we parked there, and I think that someone had been there before we got there because there had been a fire with the ashes still burning.

I only remember bits and pieces of that night with Uncle, just driving to their parking lot. Uncle is undoing his zip and getting me to make him happy.

There was another road that we drove down; it was somewhere heading toward the back roads of Clonbinane between Wandong and Broadford. There was nothing much along these roads. Uncle knew all the back roads in Wallan, Kilmore, and Broadford to take me to. There was a house that Uncle stopped at.

The house was a weatherboard house, and it had some stairs at the front. I am not quite sure what the name of the suburb where the house was situated would come under.

Uncle had a friend; just his friend and me.

I remember the steps at this house. The house was on lots of land, and the grass was brown and dead. There were lots of paddocks, and the house was in the middle of nowhere. You could barely see the fences around the house as they seemed so far away.

I am not sure stepping into the house how many steps there were, whether it was just one or a few. At the bottom, there was like a little area with a roof. I think it was part of the house. It did not seem to have grass; it was just wet dirt.

I asked Uncle if this was the friend that he wanted to see.

"Yes, Suzie," he said, "we're just here for a little while, then we will go back to see Auntie."

Uncle wanted to do the things that we had done before at Uncle's house and in Uncle and Auntie's bedroom.

Uncle was playing with himself first, then he asked me to do that stuff again by pulling my head down to his penis, putting my hands around his penis, and rubbing it.

I have no idea where Uncle's friend was and whether he was watching or was inside. I had no idea where he went until we said goodbye and went back home.

Was Uncle running out of places to take us girls, or did he have other people like him to take us girls to? He was pure evil. There are times when I remember most of what Uncle did to me, but other times, I just don't want to.

I did learn a lot from Auntie, one of the best things was watching her make a Sunday roast. I still love to have this now. I do it the way Auntie taught me, pasting all the oil over the potatoes and pumpkin now and then. Then, use the leftover oil to make the gravy. Bloody beautiful, it was.

And now, when I light the fire pit or need to light a pot belly fire, I do it as Auntie showed me when she would light the combustion stove in their home. I would start by rolling up lots of newspaper tightly. Auntie used to squash it into little balls of paper and place it in the fire, with small, tiny sticks over it. Then put fire lighters underneath the sticks, then light them with matches, and hope for the best.

She was good at it. I knew that Uncle would never do it for her. I really did not see Uncle help Auntie at all with anything involving the house. And I cannot remember ever hearing Auntie say a nice thing about him. The only times that Auntie stood by Uncle were when he was accused of sexually abusing my sister. She was really pissed off and very angry at the time. At times, I am glad that Auntie was in a nursing home when Uncle was in a courtroom trying to plead out his charges. I think if Auntie were of a sound mind at this time and still living with Uncle, she would have died anyway. This would have broken her heart, if she did or did not know what Uncle was capable of.

I just did not really care about my voice. If saying what I wanted was going to upset my family or friends, I had trained myself for so long that my voice never mattered. Uncle never listened to me when I told him to stop. And when my dad found out, he did not give a shit either. No wonder people do not have the courage to speak up. Only to be shut down and humiliated and embarrassed by what they know about sex at such a young age.

I would always feel so small.

My husband and I lost our son in a car accident in Perth when he was only nineteen. He was coming home from a friend's house and answered his mobile phone, which caused him to lose his life.

My first reaction to this was that it was my fault. I was a bad person, and I deserved this because of how I felt about myself. This was the reason why I had never told my husband about Uncle, because of how he might feel about me after knowing what Uncle did to me.

I was told to go home and plan our son's funeral. I knew that my husband could not make any decisions; his grief was unbearable. I held off for as long as I could to make choices about what happened on the day that our son was to be buried. On that day, I regretted not having the strength or the courage to make choices for myself.

Slowly, over the year, I have come to believe that nothing was ever my fault. There were reasons why I kept going over to Uncle's house. That it was not the dress that I wore, or the way I sat on Uncle's knee. I loved Uncle, and he took advantage of me and my little sister. And many other girls were in and around the town of Wallan.

For years, my addiction was alcohol and prescription drugs. I would do anything to survive. I could have gone one way or another, being totally addicted to hard drugs or dead. I think about that night he hurt me; he was vicious and hungry for prey. I felt like my body and soul had died. When I went home that night, I stood in the shower to scrub my body. I wanted to hurt myself so that I could not feel him touching me anymore.

I only wish when I was a young girl that I had the strength to tell someone what he had been doing to me so that he would stop doing this to other girls. Maybe he would have; maybe he wouldn't have. The court system would have put him in prison for a long time if it had caught him in his younger years. From writing this book, I think that carrying shame and blame all these years was stopping me from living my best life. As I was still allowed, Uncle at the time, to control me with his voices in my head, constantly pissing me off. Now in my life, I challenge every word that was spoken to me out of Uncle's lips

Here is that shame, blame, self-worth, parts of my body that I hated going back to. It was his shit, and it always was.

A Letter to Uncle

When I go swimming today, I wear shorts and a swimsuit. I push myself at times to wear a dress. I will no longer listen to your voice in my head.

You are still in my head because I did not want to believe what you had done to me. I could not heal for fear of hurting myself again. I wanted to kill you in my head could not be free of you forever.

Slowly now, I am going to put all my shit that I took as being my fault, put it in a box, go to the cemetery where you are buried, and give it all back to you. Free of the evil bastard called the Wolf of Wallan by Martin King from *A Current Affair* that was aired in 2014.

I did not realize that what I was doing all the time was letting Uncle still choose who I was going to be. I never would admit that he was still living in my head; I was still making choices in my head as a broken child when I was an adult.

I was making adult decisions in my five-year-old broken mind with all my distorted beliefs about myself.

This always ended in a disaster waiting to happen.

In my adult world, I was still thinking like a broken teenager wanting someone to fix me. I was still somehow that five-year-old who had never wanted to talk about or deal with what Uncle had done.

I knew what I had felt like on the inside and outside of my body, so it seemed sensible to me that if somehow someone knew about Uncle, they would see me differently.

Uncle took our innocence away at a very young age, but that was just the beginning of a struggle to come for lots of other challenges.

I was too sad and angry to have a relationship with all my siblings. By the time I was older, my sister and I never knew each other; we both just tried to do our best to move forward from Uncle's abuse.

As I got older, the impact of Uncle's abuse started to show with low self-esteem, no confidence whatsoever, and a feeling of numbness to want to move out of my world.

When I was out in a crowd, I knew that people would judge me as I always judged myself, so I would do things and say things so that they would talk about me and hate me anyway, so then I could say I told you so, get them before they hurt me.

I never really knew what happiness was, so to me, happy was someone who was never going to hurt me or physically abuse me. Or make me do things sexually, like Uncle did that I did not want him to.

Uncle not only stole my innocence; he stole my identity. I do not remember things that should have been my most precious memories of my childhood. He took them from me.

As much as I tried to recognize how I was feeling, whether it be sad, happy, angry, or anything else, I had learned how to push them away and not feel anything. It took me many years to learn to trust people, to hug my friends a really feel a hug, not to hug them like a stiff person who is so scared of letting anyone in.

There was so much that I had to deal with. The hardest one is that you are embedded in my body and my skin, so whatever I did or how much therapy I had, you were still in my body. Going back to my childhood now is what I am doing. I am forgiving the little girl in me that I have punished all these years for what you did to her.

I have one photo of me when I was at school that I could never look at because to me, this little girl wasn't me.

I never wanted to be a sad girl or to feel very small. I had hopes and dreams, even when I was five. But when you started to sexually abuse me, Uncle, I could not think of anything anymore.

On the hidden side of the Wolf of Wallan, you abuse your victims without any care or remorse in your world. How many over the years we will never know. You were an evil drunk who, at first, would be at the local pub flashing your money around, buying the locals' free drinks until you were so drunk that you were unable to stand. Then, when you got home and hit Auntie because you wanted to fight with someone, you would forget about everything in the morning, carry on like you were that respectful kind member of the community again. And the pattern would continue, Auntie would just keep on saying that you were a pig of a man.

I remember every year on my birthday; you would shower me with gifts and money. Auntie, at times, was not happy with how much attention and money you spent on me.

There was always going to be a price to pay for when you were nice to me.

When you were drunk one night when I was at your house, I got scared you wanted to fight with your boys. I think in your brain, you would lash out at people because you knew what you were doing to others. was evil, you never wanted to stop yourself. When you were in your evil, drunken mind, hitting and bashing people that you were meant to care about was what you did.

Uncle was keeping his control by keeping close to our parents, knowing that when we were little, he would threaten us that if we did not do what we were told, he would hurt or kill our mum and dad.

Even though my little sister Tracey and Mum had moved away from Wallan, Uncle kept his control of my sister by writing her letters, telling her to be a good girl, and making sure that his secret was kept safe.

I had moved away from Wallan as well when I was older; for me, it was only Auntie that kept me from telling my secret. Uncle thought that he could keep control of us and his secret, as long as I had Auntie in my life.

Every time I was upset when I was married and became a mum, or things just became too much, Auntie was the first one that I would ring for advice. Uncle would talk to me just for a little while to make sure that his secret was still intact.

He would always finish by saying, "I love you, Suzie boozy, bye love."

I am sure that as he got older, he would never have thought that all of us girls would finally get our justice and make him accountable for what he had done in our childhood. This would have never been possible if I had not gotten a phone call that day from a family member who was relentless in her pursuit of him being locked up for life.

I was constantly making phone calls to make sure that the police in Seymore had arranged for me to make my statement. And this went on right throughout the court hearings, having lunches together, and attending all uncle's court cases. When Uncle died, I have not heard from her since. It was not easy for us girls to face our demons and to face Uncle in court to tell our story of what he had done.

When Auntie was talking to me one day, she must have been feeling sad, and Uncle was never anyone that she could talk to.

She was talking about her pregnancy and when she had delivered her daughter, Jackie. She had these photos of Jackie in a small box in her room.

She passed away after her birth because of brain bleeding. Auntie was devastated; she asked if I would like to see them. Poor Auntie, she had longed to have a girl.

I know that I should not think like this, but when I see a picture of that beautiful little girl, I think there is a reason why this happened. Would have Uncle done bad things to her as well, as there were never any boundaries in his world.

Uncle was indicted, waiting for his sentence to play out. He had a heart attack the week before and passed away.

The only thing that I would have done, that I regret, was not speak up sooner and come forward to the police about Uncle. That would have stopped him from hurting other girls. The childhood sexual abuse that Uncle put us through didn't stop when Uncle stopped. This continued throughout my life, to not take opportunities for fear of being stupid, for fear of not ever being good enough for anyone. For not remembering all the good things in my life, only the abuse. It was just too exhausting purely surviving the

Wolf of Wallan and the damage that he had done to have ever known what being happy was ever going to look like.

For me, I never needed much to be happy. I never wanted to be frightened of you ever again in my life or never let you control a decision that I was making for my future.

When I first saw you in court in your first hearing, I knew that I had taken my power back, and I was starting to feel good about myself again for the first time in years.

My voice was going to be heard, and this time, you had no control over it. Now, I also dare to put my voice from my childhood in a book; something I have always wanted to do.

I was always frightened of speaking in front of crowds, in fear of being laughed at. But when I started TAFE, you were never going to rob me again of learning. I stood and gave my presentation, sounding like I was close to tears and shaking like a leaf.

You did not beat me that day, Uncle. With me being afraid, I was not going to give up my life anymore for you. I was so proud of myself for pushing through, even though I did not want to.

I would encourage anyone to finally have a voice, whether it is to the police or someone they trust. Sometimes, there is never a right time. I found that the more I talked about it, the more I wanted to. They say that you cannot fix what you don't acknowledge. Something that I continued to run from all my life was the memories of Uncle. I did not want to accept that someone I loved so much as a child could do what he did to me. I had come to know what my body felt most of the time that Uncle and I had been on our drives, or in all the places he took me. The night at the telecom compound when I was thirteen, it just would not let go and leave me alone. I have never been able to get this out of my head. I think it is because I did not want to believe or accept that Uncle was a monster. The trauma of this one night was so hard to talk about. I can always say what happened in my mind, but it sickens me with shame and humiliation to hear the words escape from my mouth. Uncle, I remember parts of that one night when I was thirteen, that night when I went to ring my mum.

I think what was so different about that night, there were many nights when you took me there. Was it that I was developing into a young lady? I had breasts, and I was getting taller. Tonight, Uncle, I do not remember how my clothes got off me, whether you asked me to take them off or you did it for me. I know you had nothing on from your belly down. I never want to look or remember anything that happened; I just remember how I felt after.

I was detached from my thoughts and feelings as a teenager, confused and knowing that you had done something that night that was bad.

I had learned to detach from my thoughts and feelings. I found it so hard to fully process the good in anything that was happening to me, in anything in the future after I left Wallan that would come my way. When I was diagnosed with PTSD, I knew that I was trapped in my past, a past of sexual, physical, and mental abuse by Uncle. I was relieving the distress that I had experienced at the time in my mind but still could not speak out. Uncle was chaining me down. I had chains on the inside, and Uncle controlled every move that I was making.

That night when Uncle did a horrible thing to me, I created in my mind that Uncle and Auntie's were a beautiful family; he was my Uncle and, in my mind, I blocked everything out in my head about what he was doing to me so when I did grow up, in a sick way I could still love him.

Uncle was so good at keeping his victims close to him that he knew that his secret would be safe.

Even when he was caught doing bad things to my little sister, he still did not have any remorse or care about the person who caught him in the act. He just used his violence and physical abuse to keep them quiet. As I grew older and started to speak to my sister about things that Uncle did and had been doing to several people that I knew in the town. I knew that the fear of being hurt, or others that we cared about, would be hurt was his main power in his abuse.

Uncle had a privileged life; he had a great job; he was earning good money, a beautiful, kind, and caring wife, and a family to provide for. I will never understand how his evil mind worked. There was a time when I heard pop talking to Uncle. They were having a heated discussion one afternoon when I was over there to visit. I was trying to listen to what they were saying. Pop was yelling and saying things about Auntie. Uncle always responded with a lot of bullshit to keep the scent off him. But there was one person in that house who knew that Uncle was a little strange. Every time he would visit with pops, there was one person who was always anxious and a little nervous to see him. People who might have known what Uncle was up to were never going to tell or make him accountable for his actions. They would never have been the reason why he spent the rest of his life in a jail cell. In Uncle's world, there was never anyone who was going to make a statement against him.

This book is a way of having my voice and finally getting you out of my head and my body.

I held my pain inside until I no longer could. I chose to bury my pain in alcohol, and I thought that alcohol was my problem. The problem was that I no longer knew who I was. I did not give myself long enough to like myself.

I want to go to horse riding lessons, join a club. Buy my own helmet, and Jodhpurs.

Dress like I did when I was young and feel the excitement I used to have when riding. I want to travel to a property that has a huge muddy dam on it and run and jump in. Swim from one end to the other, put my head underneath the water, and let all the shit that you put me through go. Learn to retrain my brain, feeling clean even in muddy water.

It is almost like the little girl that I buried in my mind; I am now able to set her free. I do not despise or hate her anymore.

We are now becoming one person because I no longer blame her for what Uncle did.

I spent so many years focusing on the pain, which meant that I was always going to suffer in my life. My focus now is healing, to be there for that little broken five-year-old child when no one else is. She is me, the sixty-year-old me, this is now my story and my voice that I never got to say to anyone when I was a child.

I am okay being me.

You were an evil monster of a man, not deserving of anything that may be named after you. You shattered the town of Wallan with your evil, sick fetish for abusing young girls.

You used to play football for Wallan in your younger days. Lots of people used to tell me stories about how good you were. I bet this was another opportunity for you to be around young girls and earn the respect of their parents before making your next move. You loved going to community gatherings. I remember when I would say that I had family days at school and Mum and Dad could not make it. You would say to me, Auntie, and I will come with you and make it your special day.

Auntie would take lots of lollies for the children at times when we had things that were on at the ovals. Auntie would lay her rug down on the grass, put everything in its place on the rug. And some of my little girlfriends would come and join and sit down on the rug next to Uncle.

Uncle, you took my body from me to play with for your sexual pleasures in my childhood. Never did you take my soul or my ability to keep moving forward, knowing that one day I would be free of you and able to finally have my voice.

It has always been important to me to share my story in my hometown of Wallan; it is where I grew up; it's where Uncle took my innocence from my sister and me.

I am proud of myself. I survived you; you didn't beat me down whenever I heard your voices trying to destroy me in my head repeatedly. No matter how far down I got, I came back stronger than ever.

Although you have been dead for a long time now, I was never free of you. You were never deserving of your reputation. Some people looked up to you; they trusted you. One thing that you were good at was talking about your charisma charming at first, when you were working on your plan of attack.

Coming through the pain and trauma that you caused me as a child, I am a stronger person and more resilient, realizing that some people were in my life who were just pure evil.

The Wolf of Wallan, an evil man, a child sex offender, a physically and mentally abusive man.

This was you.

As I was growing older and had more time in my life with my kids growing older, I was constantly reliving the traumatic events in my sleep.

I would try everything that I could to avoid them.

I could never seem to enjoy anything anymore; things that I used to love had come to mean nothing to me. I could not feel that feeling of happiness anymore.

I was experiencing fear in my dreams. It always felt better when I felt numb, no feeling, no body.

I know that I was developing distorted beliefs about myself, and they became very true to me.

I no longer wanted to get close to anyone and let my barrier down, as this world that I was living in became very unsafe for me.

With my depression, I felt completely lifeless, my stomach felt like a brick was lying on top of it, and the shaking in my body was endless.

I did not think I would ever learn how to relax again.

But like many other people in Uncle's family, they just went along with things and never challenged him until he was facing charges of child sexual abuse. And still, with some people, it was okay to keep visiting him and continuing a relationship with him, knowing what he had done to many girls in and around the town of Wallan.

CHAPTER TWELVE

By my teenage years, I was carrying more than any young girl should. The abuse hadn't just stolen my innocence — it had stolen my trust, my confidence, and the simple belief that I was safe in the world. I walked through school hallways feeling like an outsider. My classmates saw only the surface — the girl who was loud, reckless, maybe even wild. They didn't see the fear that lived under my skin. They didn't know how many nights I lay awake, reliving what Uncle had done, convinced it was all my fault.

Every choice I made back then came from pain. Drinking too much, laughing too loud, pretending to be tougher than I was — it was all survival. I thought if I kept people at a distance, they couldn't see how broken I felt inside.

But the silence was heavy. Carrying his secret meant carrying shame that didn't belong to me. I blamed myself for the way I felt, for the things I couldn't explain. I hated my body, hated my reflection, hated that I couldn't just be a "normal" girl.

Even with all that darkness, there was still a spark inside me that refused to die. I didn't know it then, but that spark was my strength. It was the part of me that kept going, the part that whispered: One day, you will not feel this way forever.

Uncle may have taken my childhood, but he didn't take my future. I was still here. I was still standing. And I was learning, little by little, that survival itself was proof of my strength.

CHAPTER THIRTEEN

As I grew older, the silence inside me only grew heavier. I wanted so badly to be like everyone else — to laugh without worry, to feel safe in my own skin — but Uncle's shadow followed me everywhere.

At school, I sat in classrooms pretending to listen while my mind drifted to darker places. I compared myself to the other girls and wondered why I felt so different, so broken. They talked about crushes, dances, and dreams for the future. I carried secrets that weighed more than I could bear.

On weekends, I played the part of someone carefree. I drank too much, laughed too loudly, acted tougher than I felt. On the outside I was the girl who looked like she didn't care. Inside, I was crumbling. Alcohol became my mask, my shield against questions no one asked but I was sure they could see written on my face. I longed for someone to notice. For someone to ask, Are you okay? But no one did. They only saw the surface — a girl making reckless choices, never the child still trying to survive.

Uncle's voice stayed in my head, telling me I was worthless, that no one would ever want me, that I was only good for being used. For years I believed him. I hated my reflection, hated my body, hated the silence that kept me trapped. But deep down, something still refused to give in. A spark of hope, a whisper inside me that said: One day, you'll break free. One day, you'll tell the truth.

For now, I wore the mask. For now, I survived. But survival was already proof that Uncle hadn't won

CHAPTER FOURTEEN

By fifteen, I was carrying secrets that weighed heavier than any school bag on my shoulders. I walked through the world pretending to be strong, pretending to be fearless, when inside I felt small and broken.

Uncle's voice was still in my head every day — telling me I was dirty, that no one would ever want me, that I was nothing but his to use. I believed those lies for far too long. They shaped how I saw myself, how I let others treat me, how I thought my life would always be.

At school, I slipped further behind. I had once loved learning, but now I couldn't focus. My mind was too full of fear and shame. Teachers judged me. Friends whispered. No one ever asked why. They only saw a girl who was failing, who was acting out, who was reckless. Nobody saw the truth — that I was surviving.

I turned more and more to alcohol, desperate to numb the ache inside me. Drinking gave me a mask to wear, even if it only lasted a few hours. It let me laugh when I wanted to cry, it let me feel like I belonged for a little while. But afterwards, the shame always came back stronger.

I hated the reflection in the mirror. I hated the body that carried so many memories I didn't want. I felt trapped inside myself, as if I was living two lives: the one people thought they saw, and the one I couldn't escape.

But even in that darkness, something inside me refused to give up. A small, stubborn spark kept me moving forward. I didn't know it then, but that spark was my strength — proof that even broken, I was unbreakable.

Uncle had stolen so much, but he hadn't stolen me. I was still here. I was still fighting .

CHAPTER FIFTEEN

By sixteen, I had already lived a lifetime of fear. On the outside, I was just another teenager in a small town. On the inside, I was carrying years of secrets that no one could see.

I pretended to be strong, but I was exhausted. I was tired of hiding, tired of carrying Uncle's voice in my head, tired of pretending I was okay. I laughed when I wanted to cry, I acted tough when I was terrified.

At parties, I drank until the ache inside me dulled. For a few hours, the mask worked — I could blend in, I could feel like I belonged. But the next day, the shame always came back, heavier than before.

At school, teachers judged me for slipping behind, but no one ever asked why. Friends saw the surface — the girl making reckless choices — but they didn't see the child underneath, still fighting to survive.

I hated my body. I hated how it remembered everything I wanted to forget. I blamed myself for his abuse, even though deep down I knew I was just a child who deserved love and protection. The shame wasn't mine, but I carried it like it was.

Yet even in the middle of all that pain, something inside me refused to give up. A small voice kept whispering: You are more than what he did to you. You are more than his lies.

Uncle took so much from me, but he didn't take my future. He didn't silence me forever. He didn't win

CHAPTER SIXTEEN

Seventeen should have been a time for dreams — finishing school, making plans, discovering who I was. But for me, it was survival. Every day felt like walking through shadows, carrying the weight of everything I couldn't say.

I was judged constantly. People saw a teenager leaving school early, a girl making reckless choices. They whispered about me, pointed fingers, shook their heads. Not one person asked why. Not one person looked past the surface to see the pain underneath.

The truth was, I wasn't reckless. I was broken. I wasn't lost — I was carrying secrets too heavy for anyone my age. I wasn't throwing my life away — I was trying to save it the only way I knew how.

By seventeen, I was already a mother. People thought it was the end of my future, but it became my saving grace. My child gave me purpose, gave me love I had never known before. Holding that baby in my arms reminded me that I could still be more than what Uncle had done to me.

Yes, I was young. Yes, I was scared. But for the first time, I had something worth fighting for. I wasn't just surviving for myself anymore — I was surviving for my child.

The judgement from others still hurt. The silence from my past still haunted me. But there was also a new strength rising inside me. I had been robbed of so much, but motherhood gave me a reason to keep going.

Uncle had stolen my childhood, but he would not steal the woman — or the mother — I was becoming.

CHAPTER SEVENTEEN

Becoming a mother so young was not what people expected of me — or wanted for me. To them, it was proof that I was reckless, that I had ruined my life. They whispered, they judged, and they never asked the truth of how I got there.

But for me, motherhood was not the end — it was the beginning. My child became the reason I kept breathing. When I looked into those little eyes, I finally felt a kind of love that was safe, pure, and mine. For the first time in my life, I had something that Uncle couldn't touch.

The outside world still carried its cruelty. People labelled me, dismissed me, and assumed the worst. But what they couldn't see was that being a mother gave me strength. It gave me purpose when I had none. It gave me a reason to fight through the shame and silence that had haunted me for years.

I was still broken in many ways — still carrying the secret, still blaming myself, still numbing the pain when it got too heavy. But I wasn't just surviving for myself anymore. I had someone to protect, someone to live for.

Every day wasn't easy. Some days I barely coped. But every time I held my baby, I felt a spark of hope. I knew then that I was more than the girl Uncle had tried to destroy. I was a mother, and that gave me power.

Uncle had stolen my childhood, but he would never take my child. That love was mine. That future was mine.

CHAPTER EIGHTEEN

Motherhood saved me, but it also tested me in ways I wasn't prepared for. I was still only a girl myself, carrying wounds no one could see, yet suddenly I was responsible for another life. Some days I felt strong — holding my baby close, knowing that love was pure and untouched by Uncle's shadow. But other days, the weight of the past crushed me. The shame, the silence, the self-hatred — it all came flooding back when I least expected it.

I was determined to give my child the love and safety I had been denied. I wanted to protect them from the darkness I had known, to break the cycle, to build something different. But deep down, I still doubted myself. Could someone as broken as me ever be enough?

The outside world didn't help. People judged me for being young, for leaving school, for being a single mother before I even had the chance to prove myself. They never asked the truth. They never saw that my child wasn't a mistake — my child was my lifeline.

I stumbled my way through those years, doing my best with what I had. Some days I coped. Other days I barely held it together. But every time I looked into my baby's eyes, I knew I couldn't give up. I had to keep going, no matter how much the past tried to drag me down.

Uncle had taken my childhood, but he would not take my motherhood. That was mine. That was my redemption.

CHAPTER NINETEEN

By twenty, I had lived more than most people twice my age. I was a young mother, still carrying the silence of abuse, still fighting to prove myself in a world that judged me without knowing my truth. On the outside, I tried to appear strong. I smiled, I coped, I kept moving. But inside, I was still broken, still hearing Uncle's voice telling me I wasn't good enough. Every decision I made was shadowed by his lies.

The shame followed me everywhere. I felt it when I walked into a room, when I looked in the mirror, when I tried to hold my head high. I told myself I had ruined my life, that maybe everyone was right about me.

But then I would look at my child — innocent, beautiful, depending on me for everything. That love reminded me I wasn't worthless. That little face gave me a reason to get out of bed, a reason to keep going, a reason to fight back against the darkness.

Life wasn't easy. There were days I stumbled, days I drowned my pain in alcohol, days I hated myself so much I didn't know how I would survive. But I always came back to one truth: Uncle had taken my childhood, but he would not take my future. I was more than his lies. I was a mother. I was a survivor. I was still here.

be silent.

THIS IS MY STATEMENT
MADE TO THE POLICE...

My name is Susan Baird. I am forty-seven years of age and live in Western Australia. I am one of five children. I am the fourth youngest in the family. I grew up in a small country town in Victoria. Wallan East. My parents worked hard to provide for my brothers and sister. My parents were busy working most of my life. I went to Wallan Primary School and then Broadford High. Wallan East was a very small county town with a tight community. Everyone knew each other; there were only around ten houses on the street. A local store, a railway station, and a pub. My parents became very close friends with a family across the street from where we lived. This family I called Uncle and Auntie; they were very kind to my family, always wanting to help them out. They were especially kind to my sister Tracey and me. Uncle and Auntie offered to help us and Dad out when they ever needed anyone to babysit us. Mum and Dad thought that they were good, kind people. My earliest memories of Uncle and Auntie were always being cared for at their home. Uncle would buy me lollies while Auntie would bake cakes in the kitchen. I felt that when I went to Uncle and Auntie's that it was like a home. I often liked to go over and play with the boys and feel the warmth of a real family. I feel like this because our home always felt empty with my parents coming and going. One afternoon when I was young, I was over at Uncle's. I was watching TV in the front room. I was lying on the couch when Uncle stood over me. He put his hand inside my shirt and started to move it onto my breasts. I was young and had not developed breasts yet. He rubbed all over my breasts and then worked his way down to my vagina. He put his hands down my pants and rubbed my vagina. He had his hands under my underwear, and he kept rubbing me. I can remember feeling all tingly and now realize that I must have climaxed because of him rubbing my vagina. It seemed like he did it for a long time, but I can't be sure how long he was rubbing my vagina. I saw that Uncle was moving his hands around his groin. Area. He had his hand down his pants, moving around. I did not know what he was doing, but now I know that he must have been masturbating. No one was around when this happened. I remember Uncle told me not to tell anyone and told me that I deserved everything that he was doing to me because I was a bad person. Afterward, he was very kind to me and promised me nice things. I loved horses, and Uncle had lots of land and two horses named Prince Opal and Missy. He promised me that I could ride his horse and that he would come to my school family day with me. One day, Uncle promised me that I could ride his horse, Prince Opal. He took me into the stable at his house. I do not remember a lot about that day, only Uncle being in the stable with me and pushing something into my vagina. I do not know what it was as I did not look. I was too scared, frozen stiff, and crying. I remember being sore in my vagina afterward. I know that something did go inside my vagina because it really hurt, and it was different from the rubbing. After this, Uncle promised he would take me for a horse ride, but because I was upset, he became angry with me. He told me off for not holding the reins properly, and I started to shake. He grabbed the horse reins and started pulling at them until he punched me in the face. Uncle told me he had slipped and that he did not mean it. Where Uncle hit me caused my face to bleed. I was always confused as Uncle would be so kind to me and then want to hurt me. One day, Uncle took me for a walk down to the dam on his property. I was only very young and small. Uncle threw me in the dam and left me to save myself. Uncle seemed to think it was funny that I was choking in the water. I tried to get to the bank; he was laughing, and it was so funny to him to see me struggle in fear of drowning. Uncle would often take me for a drive, and sometimes we would also have my girlfriend in the car as well. She also lived on the same street as Uncle and me. Both of us girls were around the same age and went to school together at Wallan Primary School. My friend and I would often play with each other after school and at the weekends. Uncle had a blue wagon car; it had a long bench seat in the front. On some drives in parking bays, he would have me in the front first to play with my vagina, then swap me to the back seat, then it was my friend who was playing the same game as me, rubbing our vagina and playing with himself. We never knew that this was happening to both of us until we all decided to finally speak up about it. It was always around dark time, and he would drive up to Pretty Sally Hill in the parking bay there. Uncle would buy me milkshakes and lollies when we went on our drives.

Uncle would put his hands down my pants and rub my vagina. I am not sure if my little girlfriend saw what was happening when I was in the back seat. I didn't see Uncle touching my girlfriend. There was another road that Uncle drove down, but I am not sure where it was. We went on a lot of drives with Uncle, but it was always the same thing happening. I would be in the front or back seat with Uncle, and then it would be my little girlfriend. Uncle gave me the most attention and, at times, my girlfriend would get jealous. He would call me his little princess.

Uncle would take me to church on Sundays, and sometimes he would take me to a night service in Kilmore. It would be just Uncle and me going to the night service. We would drive to church, and it wasn't too far for us to drive. I cannot remember where the church was, but we were all Catholic. It must have been the Catholic church in Kilmore. It was always on the way home. A parking bay pulls over to the side and molesting me. Uncle said that I was the best little girl to play with his penis and learn how to play with it in my mouth. Uncle would undo his pants; he had a big belt to unbuckle. He would take out his penis, and he would put my hands on it. I cannot remember how I played with it, but I know I had my hands touching his penis. This happened so many times; it was always the same thing. I remember being about eight years old and being at Uncle's house. They had a back room that was off the kitchen, and it had two single beds in it. I was lying on one of the beds, and Uncle came in. I just remember Uncle lying on top of me and rubbing his penis on my vagina. I am not sure how long it lasted, but it seemed like it was forever. He also did this lots of times, but this time is deep in my mind. I was sexually abused by my uncle so many times that it is hard to recount each time he abused me. I have tried to remember each time, but it just rolls into the same thing. Another time, I remember being in the stable with Uncle and he had me sitting on the bench with my pants down. I was sitting near a vice or something like that. I can remember that Uncle put some sort of object that was cold and hard into my vagina. It was hurting me. The reason I can remember this is because I hate having a pap smear and need to take Valium before I have one. I did not see what Uncle put into my vagina, but it did really hurt. Uncle said that I was a dirty person, and I deserved what I was getting. I never really knew what I had done wrong. He told me that no one else would treat me like he did. I remember from around this age, I began to feel disgusting and dirty. I also just felt different. I still feel like this today. When I was around thirteen years old, I remember one afternoon I had to come home from school. Mum and Dad had gone shopping, and there was no one else at home. I was scared as it was dark, so I went to see if Auntie was home, but she was not, but Uncle was. I don't remember what happened to me that night, but I was so sore in my vagina when I got home. I went home and bought my dog, Scooby, inside with me. I had a shower and washed myself clean, but I was upset. I wanted to stab myself. I got out of the shower and brushed my hair; I brushed it so hard as I wanted to pull it out. I put on a clean flannelette nightie and went to bed. I was still sore between my legs, and I put my hands down there. I found I was bleeding and thought it was probably the start of my period.

Uncle worked for a phone company, and there was a depot in Wallan East. Uncle had access to the depot and could make free phone calls from there. My mum had gone to Geelong to visit her family, and my uncle promised me that I could ring my mum for free from the depot. Uncle would collect me from home, and we would walk to the depot, which had a tall fence around it. Uncle would unlock the padlock with his keys, and we would sit in the office while I rang my mum. Uncle would wait for me to finish talking to my mum. When I had finished talking to mum, he would say, "You're such a pretty girl and my favorite." Then he would come near me again and start to put his hands under my top to play with my breasts. It felt strange with him rubbing his fingers on my nipples; they were hard and stuck out. I could feel something different in my body; it was a nice feeling, but I did not understand why. I had breasts now and was starting to develop. Uncles' hands were all over me. Uncle will always say it ok if it feels good. On this day, my uncle also put his fingers inside my vagina. He was moving his fingers in and out of my vagina, and I can remember that I climaxed when he did this. I was starting to realize that what my uncle was doing to me was wrong. I started telling my uncle that I didn't want him to touch me, but he started getting physical, and he would grab me. I felt scared of my uncle and would do what he wanted. I was also starting to get interested in boys, and I realized that what my uncle was doing was not normal. I was so screwed up in my head that I just let my uncle continue to abuse me. At uncle's house, there was an outside type of toilet out the back, as in them days they had no Surridge. Uncle had to empty the toilet bucket and bury it in the paddock. Uncle put a picture of me on the back wall of the toilet so anyone who went in there could look up and see it. Uncle told me that it felt good for him to shit on me. He would just look up at my photo and continue his business. One of the other little girls told me that he was angry with me. This made me feel like I was a piece of shit, and I was worthless. I was frightened of my uncle, so I would do everything that he told me. I felt dirty and ashamed of what was happening. Uncle would often threaten me but then tell me that he didn't mean it. I believed him. There are times when my mind is so numb, and I call it the dark places that I wish I could remember. I hate myself a little for that. I wish that I could remember more so I can tell the police. When my sister Tracey was around five or six years old, and I was around thirteen or fourteen, Mum was bathing Tracey when she noticed my sister was red raw between her legs. Mum asked her what was wrong, and my little sister said that Uncle had been playing with her. I told Mum that Uncle had been playing with me too, but nothing happened about it. It was all swept under the carpet. This is when it all came out. Mum took Tracey to the doctors in Wallan, but they said they could not prove penetration. My mum and my stepbrother went over to Uncle's to approach him. They were straight out with the question that Tracey said he had been molesting her. "What the fuck is going on?" my stepbrother said to Uncle.

Uncle was standing outside with Auntie by his side; he had to put on his best performance—tilt his head to one side, lift his hands to his face, and rub his jaw in disbelief. Nothing after this dispute was ever mentioned. Mum and Dad continued to be Uncle and Auntie's friends. Not long after this happened, Mum and Dad separated. I know this happened with my sister because my mum told me at the time. Because of what Uncle had been doing to me, I suffered at school. I went to Broadford High School in Victoria. Year ten was the worst year of my life. I was so confused about life. I spoke to a teacher who was a school counsellor. His wife was my arts teacher at the same school. I felt invisible. I was so frightened to expose my secret of sexual abuse. As I was already behaving badly and acting out, all I wanted to do was survive my trauma. I could no longer concentrate at school.

I lived in a caravan park with a friend when I left home. When I was sixteen, I met my partner and eventually got married. We moved into a flat together before we got married. I had been having regular contact with my doctor at Fremantle Family Clinic. He has been treating me with depression and anxiety for a long time. I have so many issues with intimacy, it scares me when my body feels like it did with Uncle. This has affected me all my life. I did see Uncle when I visited my family, as he was at my dad's house chatting with him over a coffee. Nothing was ever said; Uncle and Auntie came to my wedding when I was eighteen. I was at his house with Auntie, getting dressed before my dad got there. Auntie took photos of us on the day but did not get any of her and me for herself. My mum, my sister, and I spoke about Uncle's abuse when I was in my twenties. I later moved to Western Australia with my husband, who was in the Royal Australian Navy. Sometime around 2010, I received a phone call from a friend I had known when I was growing up and had not heard from for over fifteen years or so. I thought this was strange that someone I grew up with was calling, and it had to be important, as we were never close friends. She asked if Uncle had abused me and if I knew of anyone else who had lived in the town where it had happened. I did know of my little sister and one other little girl that I had gone to school with. It had been years since we were abused by Uncle, so I told her that I needed to phone the people involved before I could say anything. I spoke to some of Uncle's victims and asked if they were prepared to come forward and relive their childhood trauma and finally make this man accountable and punished for his crimes. Some were okay with it, and some weren't. I am not alone now, I thought. I decided on this day that I was going to make a statement and tell the police everything I knew about Uncle. All the hidden places that he took us to, the drives of the road in parking bays, and so on.

MY LITTLE SISTER'S STATEMENT TO THE POLICE

When I was a little girl, I lived in Wallan East. I lived here with my parents, Beryl and John, and my siblings. My sister Susan was seven years older than me, my brother Peter was eleven years older than me, and then another brother who was ten years older than me. My youngest brother, Jeff, was nine years older than me. Across the road from my house and down to the left was the house where my friend lived, Uncle's youngest son. We were the same age and hung around and played together. My best friend lived in this house with his parents. I called them Uncle and Auntie. My friend also had two brothers, and they also played with my older brothers as they were all around each other's ages.

This family across the road was also foster carers and had different kids every weekend. I didn't play with the kids, but they were all girls. I don't know their names. I'm not sure, but I think through manners I had to call them Uncle and Auntie, even though they weren't related to us. I was abused by my uncle, and the abuse started when I was about four or five. This would be 1974-1975. I didn't start school until 1976 and then went to Wallan Primary School. I did not go to any kindergarten. I do not remember if this was the first time something happened, but it is my most vivid memory. I was lying on Uncle's bed in his bedroom. He had undressed me, and I had to rub his penis with my two hands. His penis was already erect when he took off his pants, but I still had to rub it with my hands. His penis was hairy. I remember staring at it. I hadn't seen one before, not even my dad's or brothers. I don't recall what I'd been wearing, but I normally wore pants and jumpers back then. I remember him getting on top of me. He was naked. I cannot remember when he took his clothes off, but then he got up on the bed. Then he got on top of me, and he was rubbing his penis against my vagina. The rubbing was backwards and forwards. I think his penis was inside my vagina, lips on my clitoris, rubbing back and forth. I don't know how long it went on for, but it felt like a while. I remember feeling like a release, and it felt good.

At the time, I didn't know what had happened. I now realize I had an orgasm. He was grunting and groaning. I don't remember if he ejaculated or not. I remember him getting off me and dressing me, but that's all I remember about that incident.

I don't remember him or me talking during or before this happened.

No one else was at home, and I don't know why I was there in the first place. I believe that I would have gone to play with Uncle's youngest son, but Uncle sent him away.

Whenever Uncle finished abusing me, he would try to do something nice for me, like he would peel me an orange. I liked the way he peeled oranges. He would peel it off in a long piece, and sometimes it would look like an animal's tail or something fun. I remember many times I was in that bedroom and sexually assaulted by my uncle.

It was always the same, no one would be around, he would undress me, undress himself, and then I would have to rub his penis with my hands and then he would get on top of me and rub his penis back and forth between my vagina lips, on my clitoris, he would grunt, and moan and I would orgasm.

He would dress me, so I looked all neat, and sent me on my way. I remember that Auntie must have been messy because I remember her clothes hanging out of the drawers.

Another time, I remember I must have tried to resist him. I was pushed up against something (furniture) and threatened with something happening to Mum or Dad if I didn't do as I was told. I was terrified that something would happen to Mum and Dad, and I submitted it to him and let him do what he wanted. He undressed me and himself, and I had to lie on the bed, and he got on top of me and rubbed his erect penis on my vagina and clitoris. I orgasmed, and he grunted and moaned, but I don't remember if he ejaculated or anything like that. I don't remember if I had to rub his penis that time.

I also recall another time in the bedroom. I was lying on the bed, and I was naked except for my knickers, I think they were white. He got on top of me and rubbed his erect penis over my knickers onto my vagina area.

I think I orgasmed, but I don't remember anything else about that time.

I don't know if my knickers stayed on or came off. Again, no one was home.

I remember a time when my family was all over at Uncle's house. I think we were over there for a catch-up, coffee. It must have been getting late, and I didn't know if Uncle suggested it or not, but I wound up having a bath at Uncle's house and then put my pajamas on ready for bed. I was in the bath naked, which was strange because my mum and dad were a bit old-fashioned, my own mother would bathe me with my knickers at home, and here I was at Uncle's house having a naked bath. Mum and Dad thought Uncle was a good guy and obviously trusted him.

Everyone was in the kitchen, and Uncle came to check on me. He got down beside the bath and was finding my vagina he was just fondling my vagina. I do not think his fingers went inside my vagina; he was just fondling my vagina area.

It was very quick, and then he had to go. I remember being frightened of him, but then he would talk nicely, and I would forget until the next time.

I remember another time I was at Uncle's house. He had stables on his property.

I remember one time I was in the stable and Prince Opal was there. I remember standing in the stable, and I had a dress on, and Uncle had taken my knickers off. I remember his hands rubbing my vagina, and I had to rub his penis. He still had his clothes on, and his penis was pulled through his fly. I had to put both hands on his penis and rub his penis. I cannot remember anything more about that time.

Another time, I was in the stable, I must have come overlooking to my friend, and I was in the stable with Uncle. I don't know where my friend was. I am not sure what I was wearing, but I remember I was half undressed; my knickers were off, and I was standing. He was kneeling, and he had just started to fondle my vagina when my friend came into the front of the stables and saw what was happening. Uncle started yelling and ran after him and grabbed him at the entrance to the barn. He hit him across the head a couple of times and took him away. I stayed there, and I was really scared. I didn't move.

I was frightened about what had happened to my best friend. I was terrified that Uncle had killed my friend, but he went right off. He eventually came back, but I cannot remember what happened after that.

I remember later that my friend had an injury to his face. I cannot remember if it was a bruised eye or lip, but Uncle made up a story about it happening another way.

I remember another time I was in the stables with Uncle, and I was lying on the hay. I felt dirty because the hay was everywhere, all over me, sticking to my back. I was naked, and Uncle was on top of me, rubbing himself on my vagina. I'm pretty sure he just had his penis out of his pants because the stables were outside, and it was risky; anyone could have walked in. I do have a memory that every time he rubbed up on my vagina, I orgasmed.

I remember that Uncle worked for telecom. He had an office at the PMG premises in Kilmore and an office area in Wallan East. Sometimes my mum would go away for a day or two to visit family in Geelong. Uncle would sometimes offer to take me to his work at these times, and I could ring my mum. We had a phone at home, but we couldn't ring STD.

One time, he took me to the Wallan East storage office, and he locked the gates behind us, and we walked through the gates. I rang Mum and talked to her and remember not wanting to get off the phone because I knew what was going to happen. I wanted to tell her, but I couldn't because he was there, and I was scared. I got off the phone, and when he tried to grab me, I resisted and tried to get away, and he grabbed me and pulled my arm back until it really hurt. He threatened to kill Mummy and Daddy. I submitted it, and I remember I was at the desk. I think my top half of clothing was still on, my bottoms and my knickers were off. I think he just had his penis out. He rubbed his penis up against me, my vagina. He tried to get me to rub his penis, but I wasn't cooperating, and he just rubbed himself on me. That's all I can remember of that, except that he was very angry at me, even when we were walking home, he was angry, saying things like "You're a bad girl." This happened other times there as well, but they are the same memories. It's difficult to sort one from another. One time, I remember being in the Kilmore office with him. He had locked the gates after we drove through them. I remember being on the floor in an office. I was probably half-naked, and he was still clothed with his penis out of his zip. He rubbed himself on my vagina /clitoris area, and I orgasmed, and that's all I can remember. These times when I went to his workplace must have been on weekends because no one else was around. I remember a feeling of dread would come over me when he locked the gates because I knew what was about to happen.

Whenever the abuse finished, he would help me get dressed and tell me what a good girl I was, to get back into my good books before he let me go home. I cannot remember his words, but he would tell me I had to keep this to myself and not tell anyone. Somehow, Uncle was involved in Brownies/Scouts. He offered to take me to see what it was all about and whether I liked it or not. Uncle picked me up and we drove off to some bush area out of Wallan. I cannot remember if my best friend was there or not. It was a Brownies and Scouts camp together because they were not big groups. During the day, we played games and did lots of great stuff. At nighttime, we sat around the campfire. I remember all the adults at nighttime were men, and they started with the children. I saw the men undressing kids, and some of the men were naked as well. Some of the men were fondling the boys, then Uncle took me to the tree area, undressed me and himself, and started rubbing his penis against my vagina /clitoris. I think I was lying down. I cannot remember anything else about it.

I went home the next day and told Mum that I never wanted to go back. I didn't tell her why.

When I was about eight, my mother was either dressing or undressing me. She saw my vagina was red and said, "Why is your doit (her name for vagina) really red?" I told her that Uncle did it. She asked how, and I told her that he rubbed it with his penis.

Mum then organized for me to go and see the doctor straight away. I went to the doctor's surgery in Kilmore. My stepbrother Rob drove Mum and me. I do not know where the surgery was, nor do I know the name of the doctor. The doctor was male, and I know that the doctor said it was inflamed and there could be several reasons why; however, there were no signs of penetration.

Both my mother and Rob confronted Uncle about it, but I was not with them when they did it. I wasn't allowed to play with my best friend, Uncle's youngest son, for a while, then Uncle came over and said that his son missed me, and I missed him, so could I go over there, but my mother and brother would come with me. One time, Uncle was saying to Mum that it was just a misunderstanding. It wasn't. Susan and I piped up from the sandpit and said, "No, it wasn't."

Soon after my parents separated, I eventually moved away with my mother.

I have never permitted Uncle to touch me in any way. I know when it was happening that I orgasmed, but I had no idea what it was; I just knew back then that I liked it. I had no control over it.

MY VICTIM IMPACT STATEMENT

I had been judged my whole life—judged for dropping out of school, judged for drinking too much, judged for being "the troubled girl" in town. But no one ever knew why. No one asked. They only saw my choices, not the reasons behind them.

When I finally stood to give my victim impact statement, it wasn't just for the court. It was for me—for the little girl who lost her childhood, for the teenager who blamed herself, for the woman who carried his secret far too long.

I told the truth. I said he had stolen years from me—years filled with fear, shame, and silence. I explained how I grew up believing I was dirty, worthless, and unlovable because of what he did. How I froze in relationships, how I hid behind alcohol, how I carried self-hatred into every corner of my life.

I told the court that he had been trusted—by my parents, by the community, even by me. He wore the mask of a good man while destroying the lives of children. I told them how he manipulated us, how he laughed when he hurt us, how he convinced us that we were to blame.

I made it clear: he did not just abuse my body. He stole my sense of safety, my self-worth, my ability to believe in love. He left scars that no sentence could erase. But I also wanted him to hear this: he did not break me.

Yes, I endured years of physical, sexual, and emotional abuse. Yes, I lived with the darkness of his control. But I survived. I stood in that courtroom as a grown woman with a voice, no longer a child silenced by fear.

Looking at him that day, I didn't see the powerful man he once pretended to be. I saw only a pathetic, aging coward—stripped of control, finally forced to face the truth.

My victim impact statement was not just about what he had taken from me. It was about reclaiming my power. It was my chance to say, in front of the court and to the world.

VICTIM IMPACT STATEMENT

Thinking back, I do not remember much of my childhood that was not dark. Sometimes my memories are black and very deep, and other times they are grey and scattered. When I was around five, I saw myself in pretty dresses and felt so happy being around my family. We lived in a very small town called Wallan in country Victoria. Mum and Dad were hard-working people, and my memories seem to be that they were either at work or just coming home from work. I do not remember a time in my life when I felt so alone, even though I had three brothers. I was five when Mum and Dad became very friendly with a married couple who lived on our street. I called them Uncle and Auntie; they also had three boys of their own. Auntie gave birth to a little girl, but she died of a hemorrhage shortly after she was born. I don't think Auntie ever came to terms with it. Mum and Dad, and the other couple, seemed to enjoy each other's company, laughing and joking when they were together. Then, I started to spend more and more time at Uncle and Auntie's place. Auntie was so kind and loving toward me. She would sit for hours and brush my hair. I loved being cared for.

I remember craving attention, especially my dad's. When my parents were at work, I would run across the road as fast as I could for a little attention. I knew that Auntie would be cooking in the kitchen. Auntie made cookies, and I could not wait to pinch them as soon as they came out of the oven. Auntie and Uncle's house seemed full of laughter, and sometimes, I would play with one of their boys as he was near my age. I felt happy and safe at their house; they seemed to be so kind and loving to me. As I grew a bit older, I spent almost all my spare time at their house. My dad was at work during the day and working in his shed at night. There never seemed to be enough time for me. I remember just wanting to be hugged. I wanted my dad's attention. Uncle and Auntie gave me so much attention, and I liked that, especially Uncle, as we seemed to do things alone more. We would take lots of rides in his car. Sometimes, we would stop in parking bays so I could drink my milkshake or eat the lollies that he bought for me. It always seemed to be after dinner and just getting dark when we would take a drive somewhere. Uncle had lots of land and horses. I loved horses, and I think Uncle knew that the horses would keep me going over to his house. Uncle would promise me so much that I remember thinking that he cared for me as much as the whole world. I thought I was very lucky and kind of special, out of all the girls, he said that I was his favorite. How wrong was I? Uncle and I would spend lots of time in the stable; he would show me how to look after the horses, and one was called

Missy. Uncle said one day that we could go for a drive to see a good friend of his, and I could get riding lessons there. The drives there always involved a stop along the way in a parking bay or somewhere off the road; no one could see what he was doing. Sometimes, Auntie would get jealous if Uncle was spending too much time with me. That upset me because I did love her and did not want to see her hurt. Most times, Auntie was kind, and I thought that she had a big heart. I did enjoy the talks we had together and all the girly stuff that we did. As time went on, I felt like I was part of the family. I trusted them, and I began to believe that the love I was getting from Uncle was normal. Then the fear started to happen inside me. Uncle already had my trust. I loved Auntie like a mother. My parents thought that I was safe with Uncle because they trusted him as well. Uncle could not put a foot wrong as far as my parents were concerned, so he was free to do as he chose with me and to me when and where he wanted. I thought less about my dad and what I thought was his rejection. I thought that love was doing what you were told, and by then, I was too scared to stop Uncle's abuse. There was no one else in my life to guide me, and I became a lost child. By now, I am used to numbing my emotions. I had learned not to show pain or sadness in my life. I felt like I was starting to become two different people with two personalities. I started to try to move forward in my life with several voices speaking in my head. I started to control the "not so nice" ones so they wouldn't hurt me, and they were tightly hidden away. I had a secret that could shatter lives in this small country town of Wallan East. Uncle was sexually abusing me; he was betraying my mum and dad's trust, and I was totally trapped in my fear. At first, Uncle had shown love to me in ways that my parents could not, but then the monster came out. The evil one—and I was too frightened to tell anyone. Uncle would always tell me that it was okay to feel his kind of love and that I should enjoy it. I never could find a safe place that I could call home in my mind. I became a drifter and learned later in life to just let bad things lie and keep the false smile on my face. When I was small, I believed that I deserved the abuse from Uncle. I had no self-worth. The abuse burned into my mind, and I blamed myself for it all. Uncle had told me it was okay if I enjoyed it, yet I felt physically sick and was so ashamed of myself. Sometimes, when Uncle was abusing me, I would hold my breath so I would not feel that tingling feeling; it was so frightening. Later, as I began to have a sexual relationship, I found I would try and hold my breath to stop it happening. Eventually, I realized the abuse was something that I was being forced to do. It certainly was not something I had learned to give out of love. I came to hate my skin inside and out. I felt that I deserved nothing in my life because I felt so dirty and so different from my other friends. My self-hatred would grow so strong, sometimes it would consume all my thoughts. It has been a long time since Uncle's abuse. For years, I have felt like I was a prisoner with locks inside me that I could never reach to set myself free. Uncle took my childhood from me and many others in the town. I never knew who I was, as I was so busy just surviving. Uncle was evil even before he started to abuse me because he groomed me for years. He spent hours taking me for horse rides, buying me presents, and taking me on school excursions. We would even go to church together; of course, he would stop on the way there or on the way home. Around the time I started high school, my behavior started to change. The cracks began to show. I was developing breasts, and I hated it when Uncle would rub his hands all over me. I just remember my entire body being tense and my fear of being hurt. By now, Uncle's abuse was having a major effect on my personality. The only thing I seemed to enjoy was high school. During years seven, eight, and nine, I remember being a straight-A student. I loved learning. Then, one night when I was around thirteen, we went across to Uncle's. He started to abuse me, and when I resisted, he became physical. I remember thinking that it was the worst time and the last time that he was ever going to hurt me again. By now it was the start of year ten for me and my grades went from an A to a C, then a D. I was lost and out of control and felt so alone. I kept asking myself what I did that was so wrong. Then I would think that it had been all my fault because I must have been a bad person. Then Uncle put a picture of me up on his old toilet outside the back of his house. He would tell me how good it felt for him to shit on me. He said he would sit out there on the toilet and think about me and have a shit because that is all that I was worth. I felt so worthless and very alone with my secret. I often think about what Uncle said about the photo and all the other things he said to put me down. He always told me that no one would want me because I was very much used to goods. He was binge drinking and had a song that he would play in his car when we were together. The chorus would go.

WHAT YOU GONNA DO WITH A DOG LIKE THAT

SHE AIN'T NO GOOD

AND THAT IS A WELL-KNOWN FACT

Then he would turn his stupid head around and laugh at me.

ACKNOWLEDGEMENT

I would like to thank my beautiful little sister, Tracey, for her courage, strength, and reliance in helping me to write this book. I know at times revisiting her trauma would have been difficult. To my husband, Gary — thank you for putting up with my crazy. At times, whatever you said to me to cheer me up was always going to be the wrong thing, but you stood by me anyway.

To our daughter, Melanie — thank you for always encouraging and supporting me throughout my journey. You always knew how important it was for me to finally have a voice.

To Detective Sergeant Julie Trimble and the sexual abuse team at Seymour Police Station — thank you for doing such an amazing job bringing this man to justice. To finally hear him stand in a courtroom and say GUILTY, YOUR HONOR was something I will never forget. To the Victorian Victims of Crimes, for all my support with rehab and counselling services. To my social workers and counsellors over the last fifteen years, thank you.

- Anette Cotton, WA
- Graham Hall, Sunshine Coast QLD
- Helen Forbes, QLD
- VVCS Tom Locke, Cannington Branch WA
- Open Arms, Rockingham WA
- Dr. Rob Park, Buderim Market Place, Buderim
- Dr. Alex Moorse, Fremantle Family Doctors, Fremantle WA

To Tammy Robeson — thank you for all your support with printing and computer help.

To Colin Ching — who, for the last few years, has constantly been leaving stickers on my computer.

THE END